ROBERT AM STERN
SELECTED WORKS

Architectural Monographs No 17

ROBERT AM STERN

SELECTED WORKS

A.D. ACADEMY EDITIONS / ST. MARTIN'S PRESS

Architectural Monographs No 17
Editorial Offices
42 Leinster Gardens London W2 3AN

ISSN 0141-2191

Design and Editorial Team
Andreas Papadakis (Publisher)
Andrea Bettella (Senior Designer)
Justin Ageros, Nicola Hodges, Owen Thomas, Lisa Kosky,
Annamarie Uhr and Pippa Hurst.

Photography
All photographs courtesy Robert AM Stern Architects except the following:
p12 Norman McGrarth; cover pp 2, 15, 20, 21, 22, 24, 26, 27 (top/bottom),
29, 31, 32 (top/bottom), 68 (top/bottom), 69, 70, 71, 72, 73, 74, 75, 84 (top/
bottom), 86 (top/bottom), 87, 88, 89, 94, 95, 96, 98, 101 (top/bottom), 103
(top/bottom), 105 (left/right), 106 and 107 Peter Aaron/Esto; pp 56, 57, 58,
59 and 66 William Choi; p 61 Lizzie Himmel; pp 62, 63 and 64 (top/bottom)
Whitney Cox; p 78 (top/bottom) Jane Lidz; pp 80, 81, 82 and 83 Jurgen
Wilheim.

Cover: Mexx International Headquarters, Voorschoten, The Netherlands.
P 2: Ohrstrom Library, St Paul's School, Concord, New Hampshire.

First published in Great Britain in 1991 by
ACADEMY EDITIONS
An imprint of the Academy Group Ltd
42 Leinster Gardens London W2 3AN

ISBN 1-85490-011-0 (HB)
ISBN 1-85490-008-0 (PB)

Published in the United States of America in 1991 by
ST MARTIN'S PRESS
175 Fifth Avenue, New York, NY 10010

ISBN 0-312-071477 (HB)
ISBN 0-312-072465 (PB)

Printed and bound in Singapore

CONTENTS

CHARLES JENCKS
ROBERT STERN THE COSMOPOLITE

Every great city produces that type of character who personifies essential urban life: the cosmopolite. Cities naturally produce variety, discontinuity, fast change and the opportunity to modify one's identity, or inherited position in life. People born and raised in the countryside who migrate to the megalopolis face an existential shock, a challenge to their identity, a question: 'Shall I buy new clothes, extend my character, become another person?' This existential problem has been acute for more than 100 years, as the novels of Dickens reveal, and as the very provocative analysis by Jonathan Raban, *Soft City*, brought to our attention in 1974. That book, deservedly regarded as a key text of Post-Modern urbanism, shows just how 'soft' the contemporary city really is: it is moulded by our fantasies and changing styles, by the media, advertisements, and the thousands of changing sub-cultures and fashions which blow through – giving it essential life – every year.

Against this sometimes senseless change many Modern artists and architects have recoiled in anger and – as Raban argues – have adopted the degree-zero style of minimum expression. They proffer ideas of sincerity and authenticity, also prevalent in Dickensian times, and pride themselves on their individuality. But ever since Oscar Wilde, the ironies of this repeated 'authenticity' have amused people, none so much as the intellectuals themselves: those whom Harold Rosenburg called, 20 years ago, 'a herd of independent animals'. Such characters never seem to change, like the urban cosmopolites, they are urban constants.

On the one hand we have the mercurial eclectic who enjoys the various fantasies, styles and cultural opportunities of the city, and on the other, the entrenched avant-garde 'resisting' this accommodation and the fashion-go-round. Both characters are essential to the city and ubiquitous; both are not found in the village, except on holiday. The former takes advantage of the myriad possibilities offered in the megalopolis, the latter rejects most of them and limits himself to a selected group of friends and types of experience. One is gregarious, smooth and operates with a face fine-tuned to each social situation; the other is reserved, frowning and a hermit with a clear moral vision. The dichotomies continue indefinitely.

However, one can say the cosmopolite is more natural to the city because he perpetually explores its diversity. Any city like New York is not so much a 'melting pot' of different ethnic groups and subcultures but, as Thomas Dewey called it, a 'boiling pot'. Melting or boiling in its diverse ways of life, its various world views, philosophies and styles, it becomes at once a horror and spectacle, a Babylon and Disney Theme park, an 'emporium of styles' as Raban calls it and an 'encyclopedia', as the 19th century called it – with each entry disconnected and set arbitrarily to the next in bewildering profusion. The city is a pigswill of dirt, pollution and death, but also the greatest collection of wonders the world can offer.

Quite simply the city is a mechanism for sustaining difference. Its epitome is Protean Man, the well-rounded courtier of Castiglione, or the perfect Renaissance Man that Karl Marx projected for the ideal Communist state (hunter in the morning, fisherman by noonday, critical critic at night and so on), or – coming down several notches – Helen Gurley Brown's Cosmo Girl 'having it all'. The well-rounded cosmopolite, the apogee of civilisation, slides by degrees into the superficial generalist with a bit of this and that. The city mass-produces this type, in all its variety, because so much is on offer and the stimulation towards difference perpetual. Hence the metropolis, especially in the information age, is quintessentially Post-Modern in its drive to produce pluralism in ever-greater quantity. The danger for Protean Man is cultural exhaustion; they say New Yorkers now even suffer from 'compassion fatigue'. City problems, cosmopolite problems.

Bob (as I have always known him) Stern is indeed overworked, but is not lacking in compassion or generosity. Of all the successful architects with whom one associates him – Peter Eisenman, Richard Meier, Michael Graves, even Philip Johnson – he is the most scrupulous and well-mannered. Like these urbanites he can be sharp and dismissive when he doesn't like an opinion or a person's style, but he is usually considerate even when directing a barb to its mark. The reason, I believe, is that his philosophy of pluralism and very wide experience of opposite cultures, have made him attentive to subtle differences, and value individual variety as an end in itself. In our talk, below, he mentions a commitment to eclecticism arising from specific building contexts: just as each sub-culture demands a certain style and sensitivity to particulars.

Hence he has been led to adopt four or five styles – Post-Modern, Shingle, Edwardian, Revivalist, even Decon – hence his cutting the cloth to suit a particular body, not some ideology. In this flexibility Stern gets the better of his competitors and peers – Meier, Graves, and Eisenman – at least conceptually. Where they repeat their signature tunes and formulae irrespective of time, place and sub-culture, Stern the chameleon is sensitive to the locale and what the client wants: where they are deductive and follow the logic of their systems rigidly, he is empirical and flexible. Their critique of Stern, as of eclecticism in general, is that one cannot master five styles and explore them creatively; variety leads to superficiality.

The difficulties they all face, the problem of success, transcend differences of philosophy and beset all large-scale production. Stern and Graves, with their '100-person firm', or Johnson, Pelli, Meier, Moore and too many other good architects I can think of, suffer from inflated architectural production. Like economic and literary inflation, it is a disease of our time, and there is no cure in sight. The logic of the situation is as obvious as it is binding. If one wants to be a successful architect and get big commissions, one must have a large office and produce a lot of uninspired buildings; otherwise the office is never big enough, or experienced enough, to be considered for the plum commissions. This is an intractable situation; a simple fact of architectural production today which underlies all building culture, a fact which the critic should recognise and deplore. Consequences of this complaint can be found below in our talk, but hereafter I will concentrate only on what I think is of enduring value in Stern's work.

First is the cosmopolitan approach itself. Always attentive to time and context, Stern has passed through at least four phases – the 'four Bobs' of our talk – while keeping a coherent centre and line of development. His buildings usually have an identifiable ornament and well-mannered grace about them, even when they are full of Post-Modern ironies. Second are the purely architectural qualities of light, space and promenade, most notable here in the drawings. Look at the plans and sections as abstractions of spatial flow and containment, of the subtle balance between Classical closure and Modern openness. They are as sophisticated as the complex articulations of the Queen Anne Revival and Lutyens from which they stem. Note the asymmetrical symmetries, the shifted axes, the little surprises which culminate a view and sequence; note the elisions of space and surface which come from the International Style. 'Learning from Stern', like Venturi's *Learning from Lutyens*, is a matter of studying plans while one walks through a building taking note of the rich contrasts in organisation. Sometimes these are obscured by the embellishments or furniture, but they are always revealed on close scrutiny.

The third contribution is the few seminal buildings or projects Stern has designed – and what architect has more than a few? The Lang Residence, 1973-4, the BEST Products Showroom design, 1979, the *Chicago Tribune* Competition Late Entry, 1980, and the Walt Disney Casting Center, 1987-9, are all projects which have informed, or slightly deflected, architectural tradition and ones which have made a contribution to the Post-Modern paradigm. By this rather pompous phrase I mean the debate on the relation between high and low, traditional and mass culture – a central debate of our time.

As the reader will find, I was rather dubious when I first saw drawings of the Disney Casting Center because its long central corridor – where job applicants had to wait before being interviewed – reminded me of Albert Speer's entrance to the Berlin Chancellery; not something altogether intimate. As built, however, the scale and mood are more domestic than I'd imagined. Furthermore, the mixture of quotes and jokes is finely balanced with architectural elements. The long skylight ramp, the corridor down which the interviewee shuffles in some trepidation, is punctuated by a curved bridge with fake peeling plaster and three delightfully fat Sternoid columns; Peter Pan and his followers fly overhead while a stately rhythm of lights and pilasters keep the whole thing from sliding into the kitsch bathos it so nearly is. Of all the 'high culture' work for the Disney Corporation so far, it manages to capture the very volatile blend of fantasy, farce, seriousness, kitsch and hard-headed business which has eluded other architects. If one must design 'Entertainment Architecture', as the Disney Corporation calls this new genre, then here Stern has discovered how to do

it without being too portentous or pretentious. It's true the Casting Center may be conventionally ugly and vulgar – on the exterior an amalgam of the Doges Palace, a Lutyens diaper pattern, blue Mickey Mouse Scuppers and an airfoil canopy – it may be a steel shed decorated with Venetian Gothic windows and the kind of gilded arches one sees on Route 66 – but it's all the stronger for displaying these signs of realism and low-cult taste with vigour and irony. There's no attempt to hide the flat, horizontal economy of the warehouse form: the shed is simply cut up and punctuated by many signs treated as stereotypes. These fantasy-types clash, intersect and bounce against each other like so many dolled-up urbanites riding a mid-town bus, or London tube; just the kind of crazy collage of instant identities one sees in an urban crowd. If the shoppers on Fifth Avenue could be turned into a building it might look like this.

Here again we return to Bob the Cosmopolite. Cosmos – 'order of the universe', cosmetic – 'order of the face', cosmopolite – 'citizen of the world free from national limitations', are all suggestions embedded in his work. It has a universal ordering system, its facades are always graced by the equivalent of rouge and it refers to every, or at least any, national style. All the exclusions of Modernism are excluded, there is no sectarianism here. In this universe the ideologies of the recent past – national, religious, cultural – have been replaced by different genres, each one to be adopted for the situation at hand. Sometimes this results in bland accommodation, sometimes it explodes into a creative breakthrough, a forceful collage whose beauty lurks behind the grotesque and vulgar. As in much Post-Modern and popular architecture, one has to look through one's first impression to see the radical idea and beauty underneath. There are several different styles and personalities which Stern has cultivated *en serie* and they have to be perceived and judged differently; no mean task for the viewer, client or indeed the critic. In a sense the 'four Bobs' I have produced out of a conceptual hat are a direct reflection of the variety of the city – its multiphrenic heterogeneity (to coin a phrase which won't be used again) – and just as one cannot come to a final or complete understanding of any large city, so his work eludes a single judgement or summary. The encyclopedia, the labyrinth, the cosmopolite are not to be pinned down in any one phrase, tradition or mood which is one reason we continually return to them – we value their elusive heterogeneity.

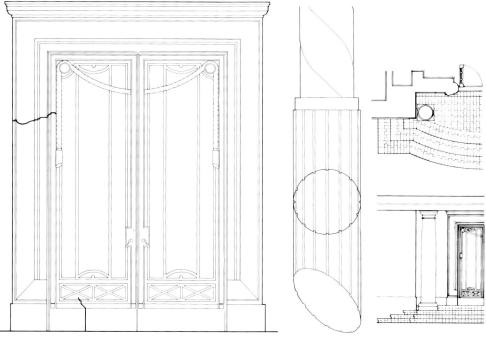

VILLA IN NEW JERSEY, 1983-89

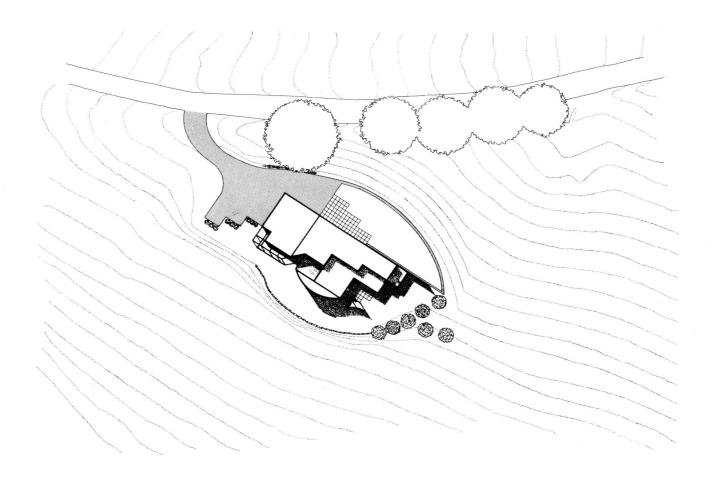

LANG RESIDENCE
WASHINGTON, CONNECTICUT, 1973-74

A year-round residence commissioned by a retired academic couple, the Lang House was designed to be economically competitive with customised prefabricated houses on the market. To accomplish this, only the facade and public spaces were fine-tuned: bedrooms and service spaces were kept very simple.

The transverse axis of the house was shifted to form an outdoor vestibule. This shift intensifies the perception of the plan's axiality and the layering of the spaces. The vestibule buffers the house from the wind and gives it a big scale. A double-height light monitor stretches

across the garden front, backwashing the living and dining spaces with warm south light; a second monitor introduces light at the rear of the living room. The curve of the principal monitor and its extended screen wall gives the house scale and frames the views from the inside. The exuberant swelling curve of the garden facade contrasts with the entrance facade, where decoration obscures and intensifies the scale. The decoration also enables us to indulge, in a witty way, an overt recollection of older modes of architectural expression. Is this a neo-Palladian Regency Art-Deco farm house?

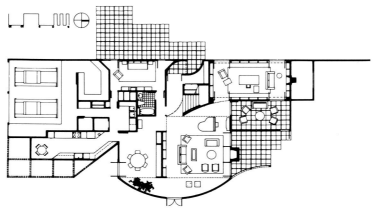

OPPOSITE: VIEW FROM WEST; *ABOVE*: SITE PLAN; *BELOW*: PLAN

9

RESIDENCE
WESTCHESTER COUNTY, NEW YORK, 1974-76

This residence and outbuildings in Westchester County focus on a wide variety of problems at the residential scale, in part because they represent an atypical programme of unusually extensive scope, and also because various strategies were required to mediate between the elaborate nature of the project and the desire for a relatively modest and unpretentious residential grouping. In order to make the house appear smaller on the inside as well as the outside, but more particularly on the outside, several design strategies were evolved in
the siting and organisation. At the entry courtyard, the facade that is axially related to the driveway is a relatively small curved segment: the main bulk of the structure is set at an angle to the line of approach, so that it is only a corner of the house that occupies the foreground.

This complex of houses is reached by a new one-half-mile-long road. The site is at the top of a steep hill; a magnificent hemlock grove and superb views of the neighbouring countryside are its principal features.

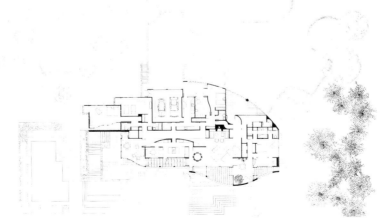

OPPOSITE: EXTERIOR DETAIL OF CURVING SCREEN WALL; *ABOVE*: MAIN HOUSE FROM NORTHWEST; *BELOW*: FLOOR PLAN

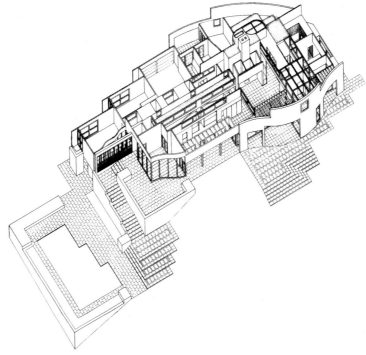

ABOVE: INTERIOR VIEW OF MAIN LIVING ROOM; *BELOW*: AXONOMETRIC

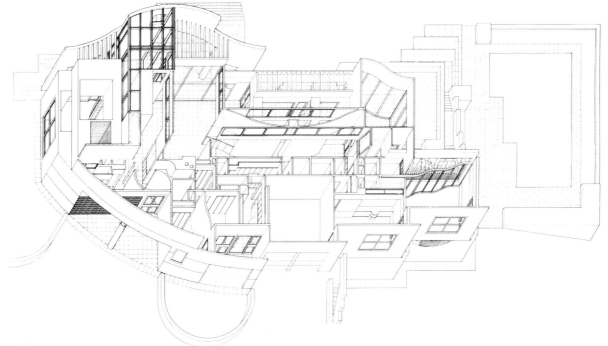

ABOVE: DETAIL OF CHANGING ROOM ENTRANCE; *BELOW*: AXONOMETRIC

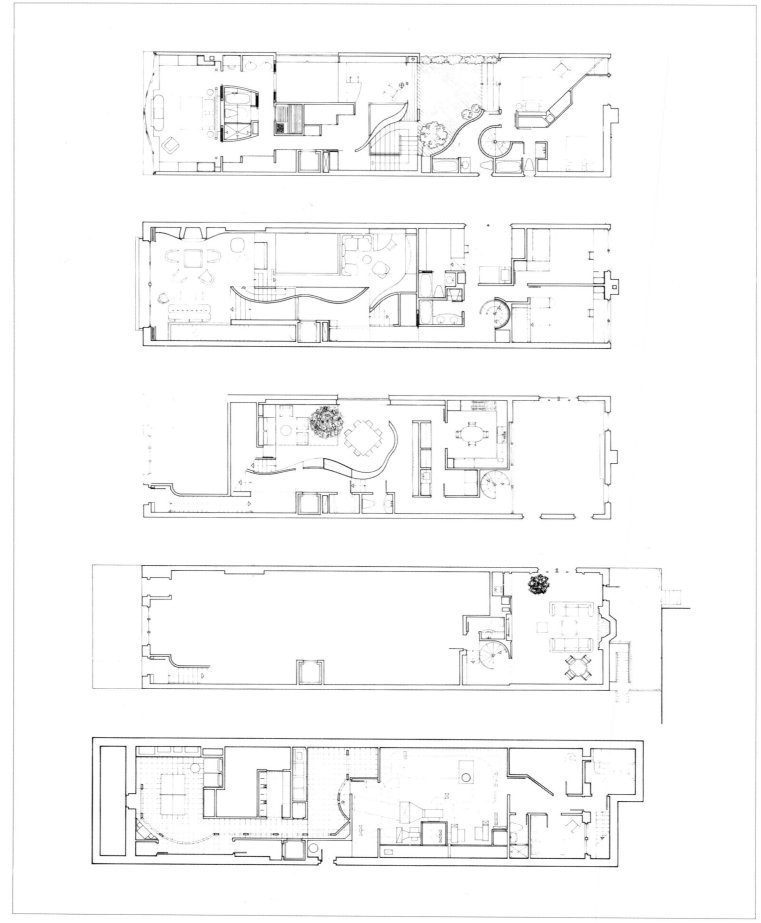

TOP TO BOTTOM: FOURTH, THIRD, SECOND, FIRST AND BASEMENT FLOOR PLANS

NEW YORK TOWNHOUSE
NEW YORK, NEW YORK, 1975

A complete reconstruction of a townhouse squeezed between apartment blocks on one of New York's most fashionable avenues, this design deals with privacy, light and orientation in a constrained urban context.

In response to the problems of scale, an abstract gridding was introduced which alludes to the base/shaft/capital schema of taller neighbouring buildings. There are intimations of pilasters at the edges, and a gradual progression in the vertical plane from solid to void, capped by a cornice which appears to be suspended from above. These strategies connect our facade with its neighbours and evoke images of traditional, Classicising townhouse design.

Inside, the major living and entertaining spaces are linked by a promenade architecturale *extending from the front entrance hall up to the master bedroom suite at the top. A circular stairway towards the rear of the building offers a more direct vertical link, while an elevator provides a third means of circulation. Because of the depth of the house, a four-storey high atrium was introduced to bring light from monitor windows above and to give an internal focus to the plan and section.*

ABOVE L TO R: STREET ELEVATION, INTERIOR VIEW UP FROM DINING ROOM; *BELOW:* INTERIOR VIEW OF LIVING ROOM

ABOVE: VIEW OF HOUSING BLOCK; *BELOW*: VIEW FROM SOUTH

ROOSEVELT ISLAND COMPETITION
NEW YORK, NEW YORK, 1975

In November 1974, the New York State Urban Development Corporation anounced an open competition for housing 1,000 upper, middle, and low income families on an 8.8 acre parcel of land on Roosevelt Island in New York City. The jury was split and, of 250 submissions, this office's was awarded one of the four first prizes.

Our solution introduces a pedestrian street 'Octagon Way' running longitudinally through the site and continuing the diagonal offsets of the street pattern established in earlier stages of the island's development. Octagon Way gives access to the apartments as well as to such various community functions as meeting rooms, a day-care centre, two public schools, laundry rooms, and an amphitheatre. It provides the principal pedestrian gateway to Octagon Park, a major park and recrea-

tional area planned for the island.

The three apartment towers are placed at the water's edge to take advantage of river views and to minimise their apparent bulk and the effect of their shadows on the usable open spaces. Almost all apartments have two exposures, and throughout the project there is a wide variety of apartment type. More than one-half of the apartments are accommodated in six and eight-storey buildings which provide residents with a comfortable relationship to the ground plane, and many have unprogrammed living spaces and private gardens, terraces or balconies. All apartment buildings enter directly from Octagon Way and all townhouse apartments have direct access to it, enhancing the sense of identity and privacy for the individual apartment dweller.

ABOVE: MODEL VIEW FROM SOUTHEAST; *BELOW, L TO R*: TWO VIEWS OF PARK AND HOUSING, PEDESTRIAN WALKWAY

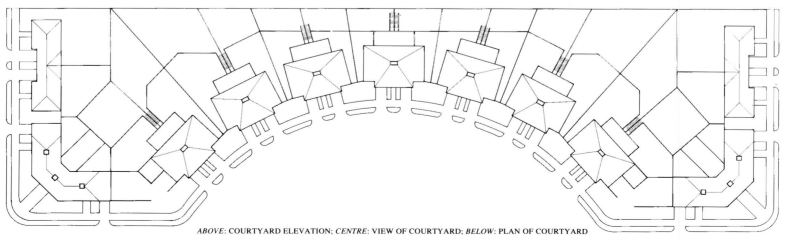

ABOVE: COURTYARD ELEVATION; *CENTRE*: VIEW OF COURTYARD; *BELOW*: PLAN OF COURTYARD

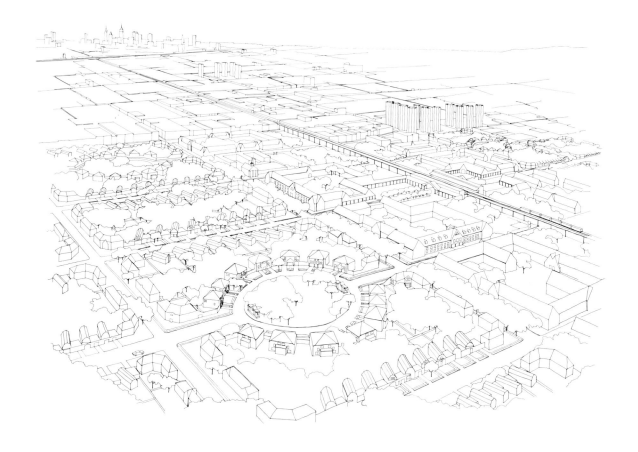

SUBWAY SUBURB

1976-80

In a purely speculative project prepared for the 1976 Venice Biennale, and subsequently elaborated and refined, a new way was proposed to build affordable communities within the confines of the city, relatively close to its centre, utilising land once used for industry or tenement housing, land now abandoned and with no apparent higher destiny or value. Subway Suburb demonstrates the continuing viability of the archetypal American urban settlement type, the modest freestanding house on a modest lot facing a street. Utilising existing road and utility grids to offset development costs, and taking advantage of existing rapid transit services and other municipal facilities such as schools, it could provide housing in the city at the densities of new moderate-priced suburban development in outlying areas, reconstituting the traditional city as both a vital place to work in and a territory comfortable with the family car and backyard barbecues. By accepting known functional paradigms and confining invention to the adaption of formulae of shapes and symbols to present-day technology, economics, and 'life-style', a workable urbanism could be established.

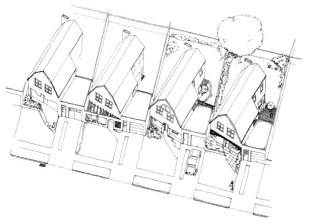

ABOVE: SITE PLAN; *BELOW*: AXONOMETRIC OF TYPICAL HOUSES

LAWSON RESIDENCE
EAST QUOGUE, NEW YORK, 1979-81

Set along the ocean beach on a typical, narrow seaside lot, this design seeks to connect with the traditions of the Shingle Style and more particularly with the kinds of 'beach cottages' that proliferated along the East Coast in the 1910s and 1920s, cottages whose stylistic simplicity and direct use of materials surely grew out of the writings and designs of Gustave Stickley. The position of the house at the edge of a dune made it possible to tuck three small guest bedrooms at ground level behind the dune. Thus, the over-scaled stoop leads up to the principal floor just below the level of the dune. It also provides an inviting porch from which to observe the sunset across the bay. The master bedroom is located in the attic, lit by a boldly arched window at the seaside that gives the house a big scale and connects it with the high architecture of Classicism, just as the eyelid dormer in the master bath pays respect to HH Richardson. Though the eroded configuration of the principal floor responds to the considerations of site, view and solar orientation, the symmetrical organisation of the mass is intended to give the house a dignity and iconic clarity of its own – an object of calm amidst helter-skelter.

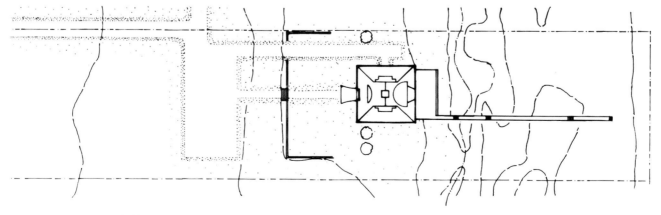

OPPOSITE: VIEW OF MAIN ENTRANCE; *ABOVE*: INTERIOR VIEW OF MASTER BEDROOM; *BELOW*: SITE PLAN

ABOVE: VIEW FROM THE SOUTHEAST; *BELOW*: VIEW FROM THE SOUTHWEST

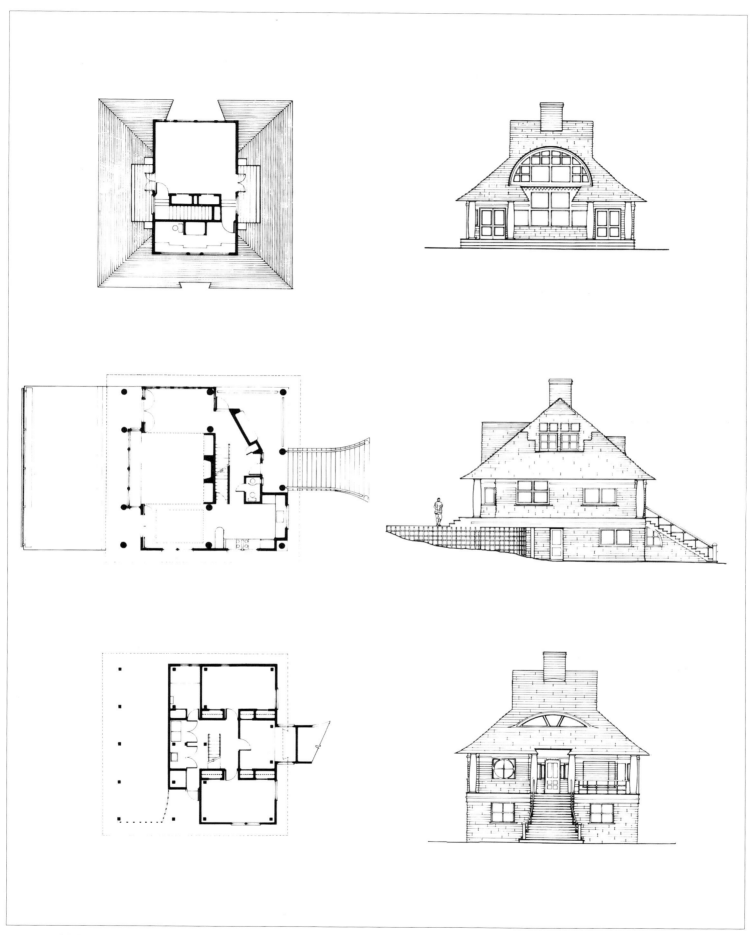

ABOVE L TO R: MEZZANINE FLOOR PLAN, SOUTH ELEVATION; *CENTRE*: FIRST FLOOR PLAN, EAST ELEVATION; *BELOW*: GROUND FLOOR PLAN, NORTH ELEVATION

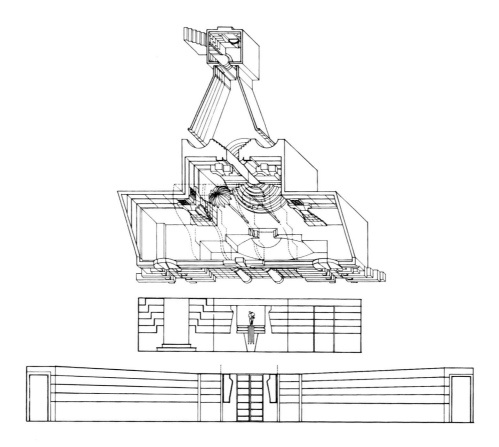

RESIDENCE
LLEWELLYN PARK, NEW JERSEY, 1979-81

This project consists of two components: the renovation of a 50-year-old Georgian house designed by Edgar Williams with the addition of a tennis court and a new indoor swimming pool.

Additional family space was carved out of former servants' bedrooms; the principal living rooms were reconfigured with space-defining screen walls threaded within a grid of columns. Thus the traditional house of 1929 was modernised through a historical approach drawing on the strategies of the International Style.

The pool house is deliberately complex in its formal references – a relaxed setting cloaked in an envelope that responds to the character of the original house, while at the same time taking on the character of a landscape feature; it is a kind of grotto or nymphaeum marking a transition between the house, its terraces, and garden. By virtue of its massive columns and thick masonry walls, as well as the proto-Classical inspiration of its forms, the pool house dips into time to provide a setting that is both primordial and sophisticated.

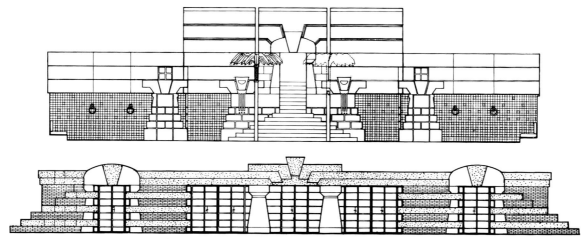

OPPOSITE: INTERIOR VIEW OF POOLHOUSE; *TOP TO BOTTOM*: POOLHOUSE AXONOMETRIC, VESTIBULE SECTION, HALL SECTION, INTERIOR AND EXTERIOR ELEVATIONS

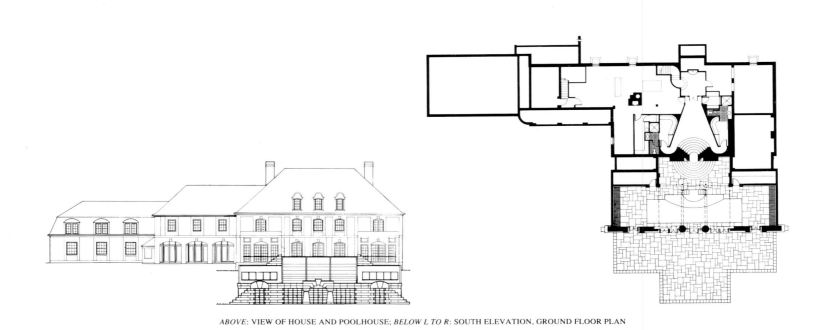

ABOVE: VIEW OF HOUSE AND POOLHOUSE; *BELOW L TO R*: SOUTH ELEVATION, GROUND FLOOR PLAN

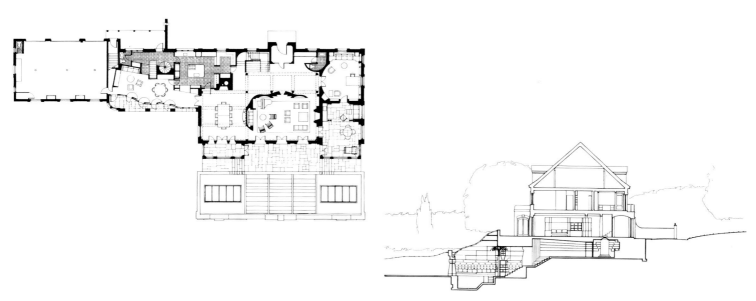

ABOVE: INTERIOR VIEW OF POOLHOUSE ENTRANCE; *BELOW L TO R*: FIRST FLOOR PLAN, SECTION THROUGH HOUSE AND POOLHOUSE

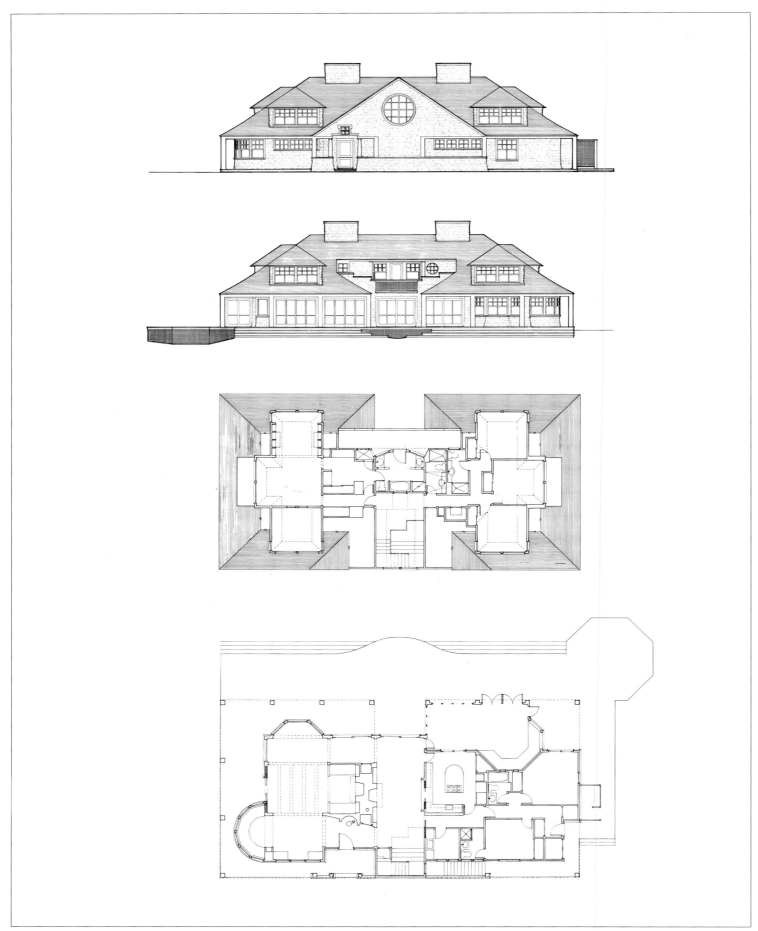

TOP TO BOTTOM: EAST ELEVATION, WEST ELEVATION, SECOND FLOOR PLAN, FIRST FLOOR PLAN

RESIDENCE AT CHILMARK
MARTHA'S VINEYARD, MASSACHUSETTS, 1979-83

Set on one of the island's highest sites, commanding water views in three directions, this shingled house with its gently flared hipped roof, dormers, bay windows and subsumed porches continues the language of traditional seaside architecture that emerged in the 1870s and has ever since defined summer-time living for many along *the New England shore. At the entrance, the roofline is interrupted by a large gable containing the asymmetrically located front door and circular window lighting the generously proportioned stair behind. On the opposite side, the hipped roofs are distended to provide a second-storey balcony overlooking the principal view.*

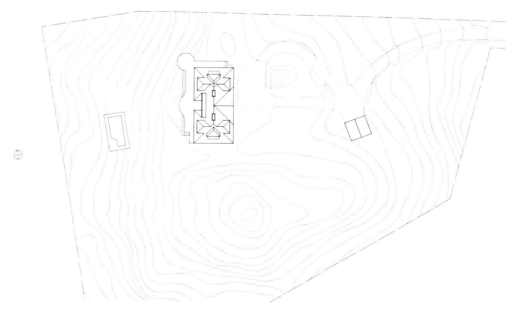

ABOVE: VIEW FROM SOUTHWEST; *BELOW*: SITE PLAN

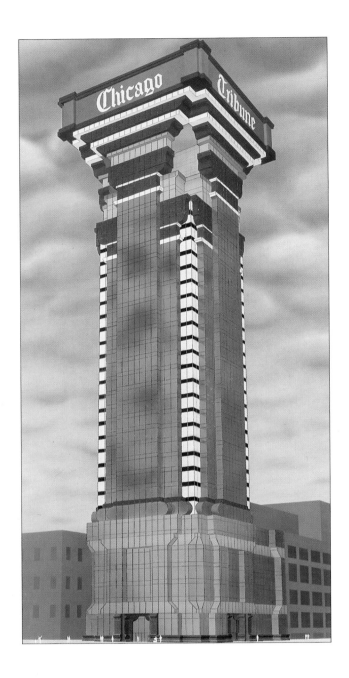

CHICAGO TRIBUNE TOWER COMPETITION, LATE ENTRY
CHICAGO, ILLINOIS, 1980

In response to a request by two Chicago architects, Stanley Tigerman and Stuart Cohen, we prepared a 'late entry' to the Chicago Tribune *Tower Competition, taking as our primary reference Adolf Loos' entry in the original 1921-22 competition, and attempting to marry that project to the Miesian prism of the same period, the most advanced expression of the steel skyscraper at that time and now. Our classical tower in metal and glass marries traditional architecture with advanced technology, a synthesis well within the Classical canon.*

The signboard at the top refers to the cultural conditions of the Mid-West which gave rise to the urbanism of the false front and to the self-serving boosterims of the newspaper's name Chicago Tribune. *Our Tuscan order reflects the presumptive moral austerity and rectitude of the ancient Roman Tribunes, as does the red and gold colour scheme.*

The signboards also recall Henri Labrouste's 'Bridge connecting France and Italy'. The word 'Tribune' announces that in crossing the river one enters the land where the Chicago Tribune *pioneered large scale development, the word 'Chicago' on the north face announces that one will soon be entering the 'real' Chicago of the Loop area and leaving behind the other Chicago of suburbs and styles, the cultural complexities of Frank Lloyd Wright, Howard Shaw and David Adler.*

RESIDENCE AT FARM NECK
MARTHA'S VINEYARD, MASSACHUSETTS, 1980-83

This house is located on a virtually flat site bordered at one edge by high trees, but otherwise open to neighbouring house lots, a golf course, and the water beyond. Our design, in response to the vast site and to the particularly complex programme, uses an archetypal gable form, looking back to McKim, Mead and White's Low House and Grosvenor Atterbury's Swayne House in the Shinnecock Hills. The clarity of the gable form lends an imposing scale which is enhanced by the near symmetry of the principal facade and the pronounced silhouette of the chimneys and dormers. On the entrance side, the projection of a smaller gabled wing serves to imply an entrance court while making the scale more intimate. The projecting bay windows open the interior to the view, while within, the use of mullioned windows helps to enrich the impact of the vast site by framing it.

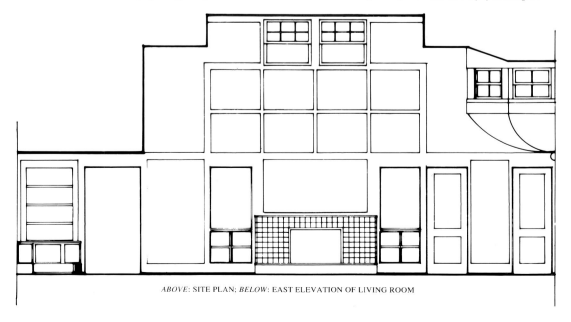

ABOVE: SITE PLAN; *BELOW:* EAST ELEVATION OF LIVING ROOM

ABOVE: VIEW FROM NORTH; *BELOW*: VIEW FROM SOUTH

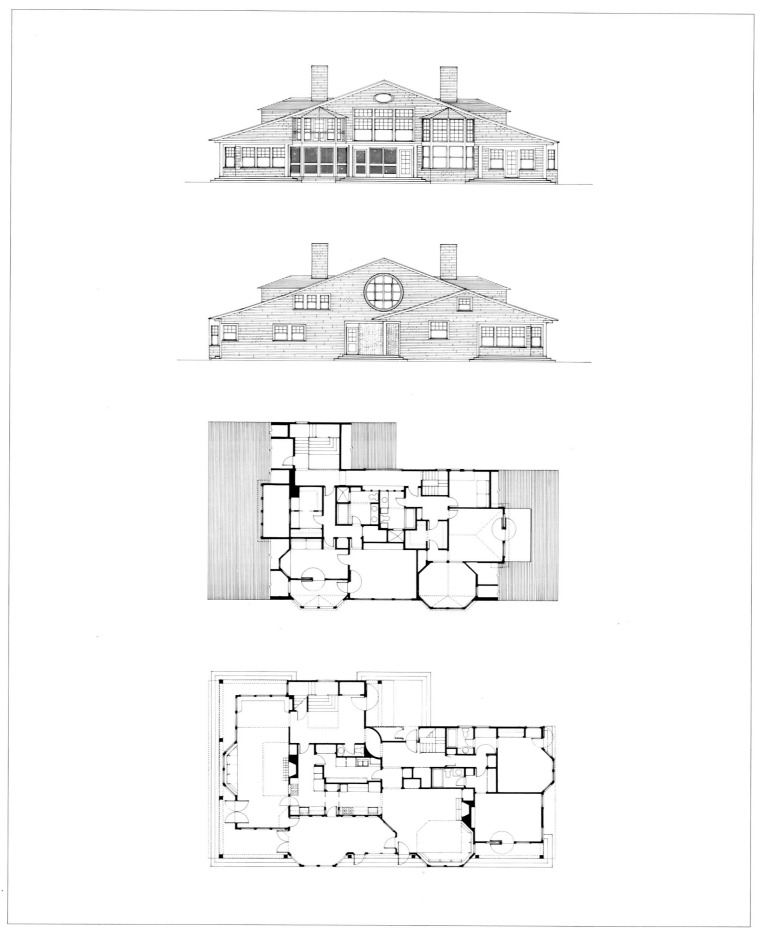

TOP TO BOTTOM: SOUTH ELEVATION, NORTH ELEVATION, SECOND FLOOR PLAN, FIRST FLOOR PLAN

RESIDENCE
EAST HAMPTON, NEW YORK, 1980-83

In the heart of East Hampton's traditional summer colony, this house takes its cues from the characteristic Shingle Style 'cottages' in the neighbourhood, which were in turn interpretations by 19th-century architects of houses built by 17th-century English settlers.

In plan, detail, and massing, this house reflects the

Shingle Style's hybridisation of Classical and vernacular elements, thereby ennobling the rituals of everyday life with memories of a grand, shared tradition. The house declares but does not flaunt its modernity; traditional forms are subtly modified, but their representational character is retained.

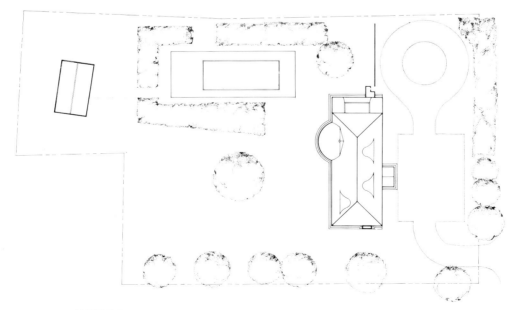

OPPOSITE: DETAIL OF SKYLIGHT; *ABOVE*: INTERIOR STAIRCASE DETAIL; *BELOW*: SITE PLAN

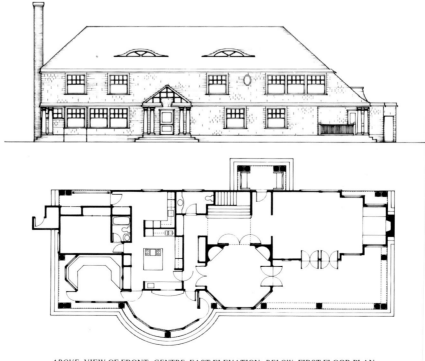

ABOVE: VIEW OF FRONT; *CENTRE*: EAST ELEVATION; *BELOW*: FIRST FLOOR PLAN

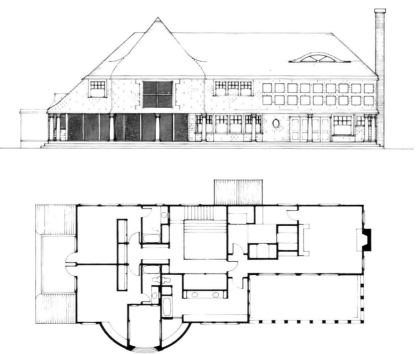

ABOVE: VIEW OF REAR; *CENTRE*: WEST ELEVATION; *BELOW*: SECOND FLOOR PLAN

OBSERVATORY HILL DINING HALL
UNIVERSITY OF VIRGINIA, CHARLOTTESVILLE, VIRGINIA, 1982-84

Porch-like additions camouflage the existing facility (1972) and ameliorate the disjunction between that building and the university's Jeffersonian architectural tradition. The use of pyramidal roofs, arches, moulded brick, Classical columns, and wood trim combined with steel-framed glazing establishes a scale and character that is at once modern and traditional; and most importantly, connected to the vernacular of the place.

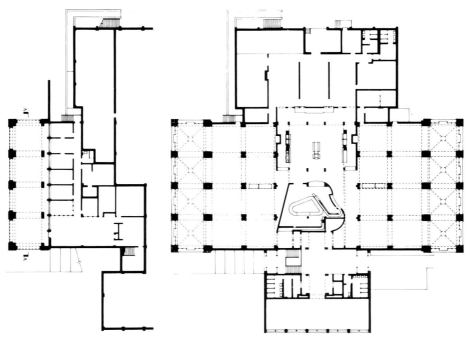

OPPOSITE: INTERIOR VIEW; *ABOVE*: VIEW FROM SOUTHWEST; *BELOW*: FIRST FLOOR AND LOGGIA LEVEL PLANS

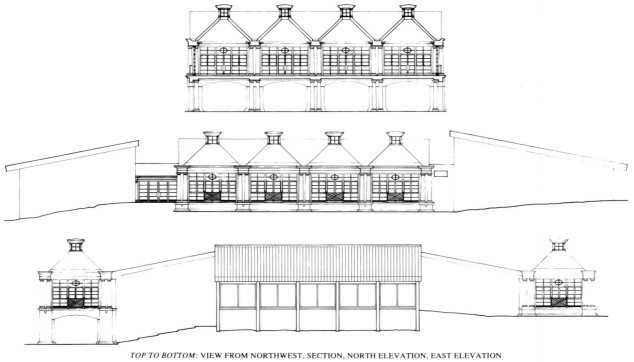

TOP TO BOTTOM: VIEW FROM NORTHWEST, SECTION, NORTH ELEVATION, EAST ELEVATION

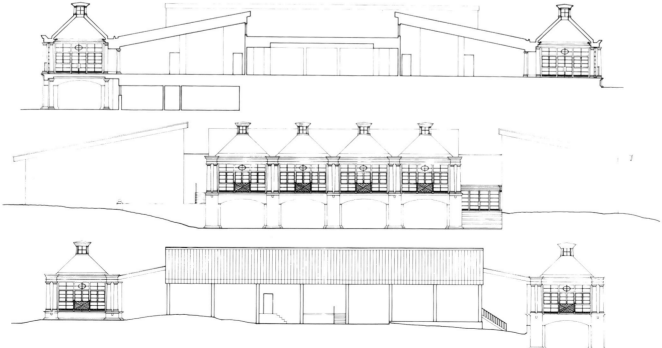

TOP TO BOTTOM: INTERIOR VIEW, SECTION, SOUTH ELEVATION, WEST ELEVATION

ABOVE L TO R: EAST ELEVATION, NORTH ELEVATION; *CENTRE*: SECTIONS; *BELOW L TO R*: WEST ELEVATION, SOUTH ELEVATION

RESIDENCE
BROOKLYN, NEW YORK, 1983-86

This single-family detached house occupies what was the only undeveloped lot in a neighbourhood largely constructed in the 1920s. The design attempts to refine the architectural themes that typify the neighbouring houses, and to establish a unique identity through the quality and character of its detailing and the rich mixture of its materials. The basement and first floor are rusticated with alternating bands of red brick and

granite, while the second floor is faced with cream-coloured stucco. Painted steel casement windows and a green glazed tile hipped roof complete the vocabulary.

Rooms are gathered about an entry hall two floors high culminating in a gilt dome. The sizes of the rooms are perceptually aggrandised by 12-feet ceilings and their arrangement along an axis, permitting space to be visually borrowed from adjacent hallways.

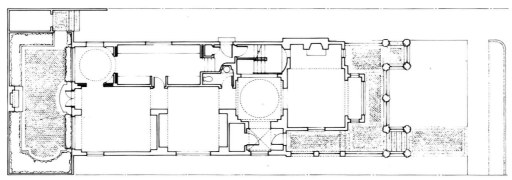

ABOVE L TO R: SECTIONAL DETAIL, VIEW FROM NORTHEAST, ELEVATIONAL DETAIL; *BELOW*: FIRST FLOOR PLAN

ABOVE L TO R: EAST ELEVATION, WEST ELEVATION; *CENTRE L TO R*: SECTION LOOKING WEST, SECTION LOOKING SOUTH; *BELOW L TO R*: NORTH ELEVATION, SOUTH ELEVATION

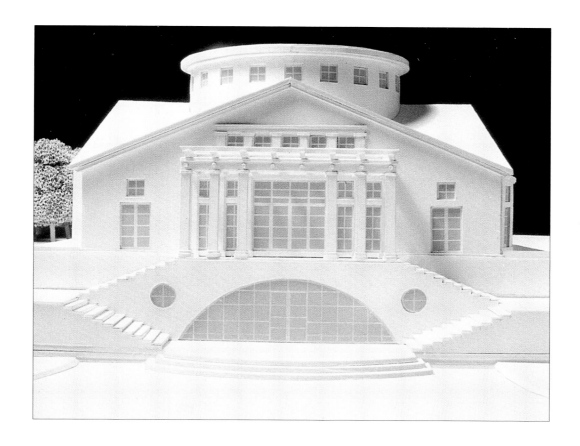

FARMHOUSE
OLDHAM COUNTY, KENTUCKY, 1983

Drawing on the 'Greek Revival' traditions of the region, this house, to have been located on a hill with expansive views on all sides, organises a complex programme into a compact square, resulting in a design that is capable of accommodating large groups of guests while remaining intimate for the owners. Most of the living spaces are on the first floor, which is zoned into three parts – the master bedroom suite to the north, the family living spaces to the south, and the formal entertainment and reception rooms in the centre. The second floor contains guest rooms and galleries to display the owner's large collection of American crafts. The round gallery in the centre of the second floor satisfies the expectation raised by the exterior massing, while the space between the inner and outer drum brings unexpected natural light into the centre of the house. The lower floor contains service spaces and a grotto-like pool that is lit by a large arched window under the living-room pergola.

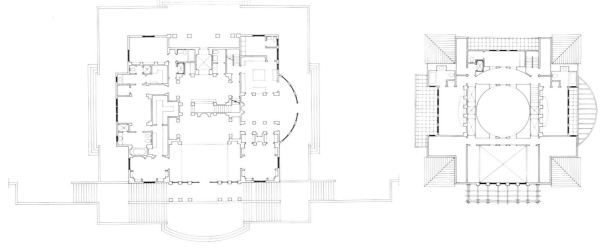

ABOVE: MODEL VIEW FROM WEST; *BELOW L TO R*: FIRST AND SECOND FLOOR PLANS

ABOVE: VIEW FROM EAST; *BELOW*: VIEW FROM WEST

POINT WEST PLACE
FRAMINGHAM, MASSACHUSETTS, 1983-85

Located adjacent to a toll plaza along the Massachusetts Turnpike, this 110,000 square feet, five-storey structure is typical of contemporary suburban office buildings, but transformed through colour and Classically derived ornament to establish a sense of place and character appropriate to its prominent site. The building's clear geometric form provides for flexible office space and gives it the scale necessary to make a visual impact on passing motorists. The polychromatic striping of the glass curtain wall establishes a more human scale and suggests the pattern of traditional stone coursing. The granite portico culminates the approach sequence which begins with a tree-lined court of honour: at once the building seems a pavilion in a formal garden and a palace of work. Behind the portico, the curve of the entrance hall draws the visitor inwards.

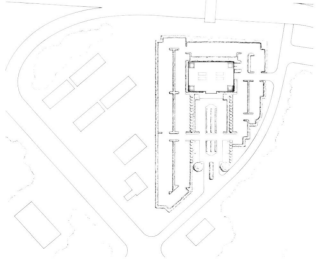

ABOVE: INTERIOR VIEW OF MAIN STAIRCASE; *BELOW*: SITE PLAN

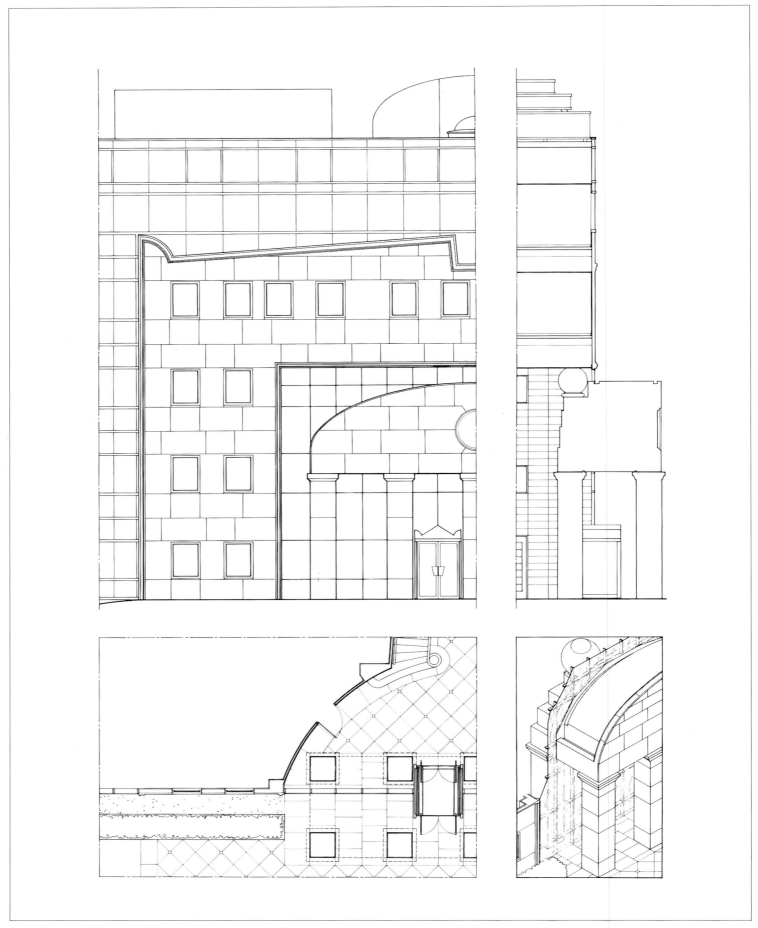

ABOVE L TO R: ELEVATIONAL DETAIL, SECTIONAL DETAIL; BELOW: SECTIONAL DETAILS

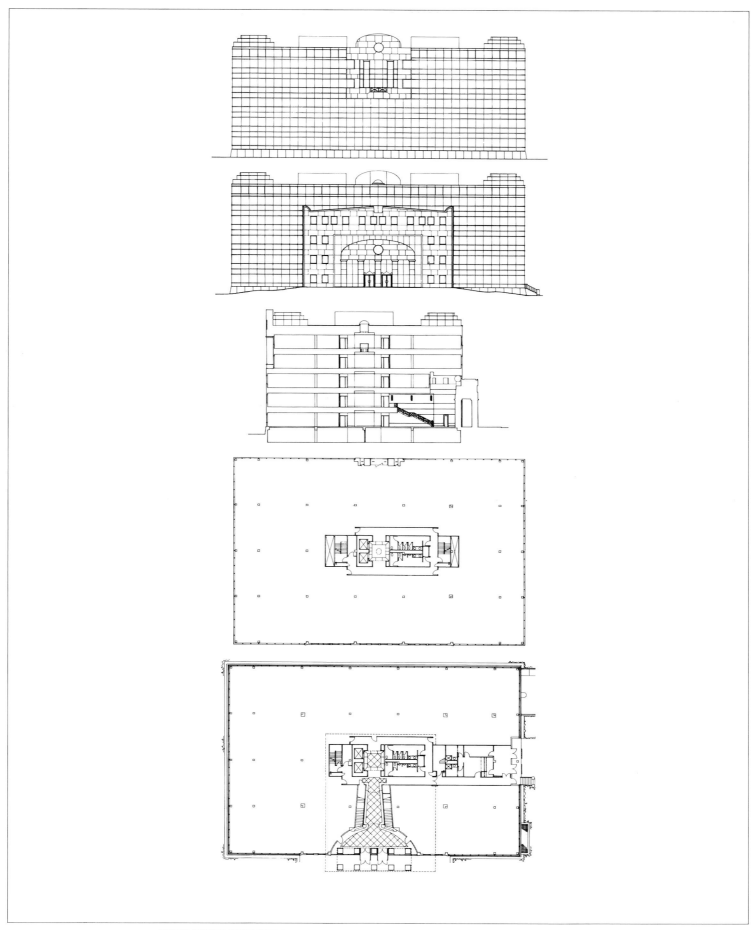

TOP TO BOTTOM: WEST ELEVATION, EAST ELEVATION, SECTION, FOURTH FLOOR PLAN, FIRST FLOOR PLAN

ABOVE: REAR VIEW OF HOUSE AND GARDEN; *BELOW*: VIEW OF FRONT

VILLA IN NEW JERSEY
1983-89

Located among the turn-of-the-century Italianate villas of a former resort colony, this house explores the integration of architecture with an idealised, Classical landscape. From the street only a narrow facade can be glimpsed through a gate. The driveway circles beneath a porte-cochère *where a garden wall conceals the service court. A vestibule leads past a long hall to an enfillade combining card, living, and dining rooms each opening up to a pergola shaded terrace that overlooks a sunken court. Framed by telescoping walls and low*

trees, a vista of grass terraces forms a cross axis stretching from the house towards a carved limestone fountain basin in the distance. Beneath the pergola terrace, a grotto-like indoor poolroom receives the axis of the sunken court and its forced perspective.

At the western end of the house lie the more informal living spaces: the breakfast room overlooks a small orchard and the outdoor pool; the double-height family room commands the axis of a flower garden leading to a secret open-air room sculpted of yew hedge.

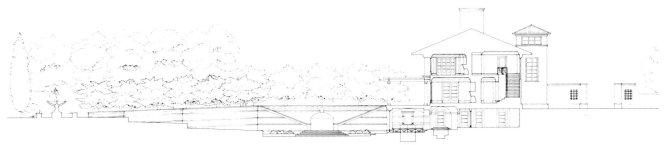

ABOVE: SIDE VIEW OF POOL AND HOUSE; *BELOW*: TRANSVERSE SECTION

ABOVE: VIEW OF FOUNTAIN AND GARDEN; *BELOW*: VIEW OF POOL

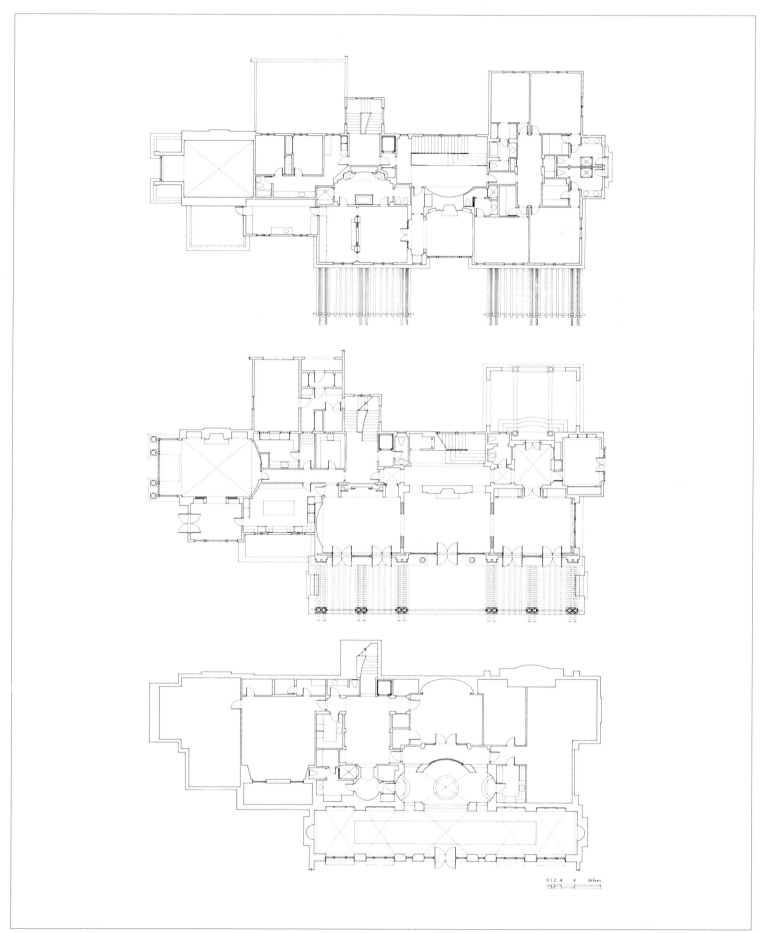

ABOVE: SECOND FLOOR PLAN; *CENTRE*: FIRST FLOOR PLAN; *BELOW*: BASEMENT PLAN

ABOVE: VIEW ALONG VERANDA; *BELOW*: INTERIOR VIEW OF POOLROOM

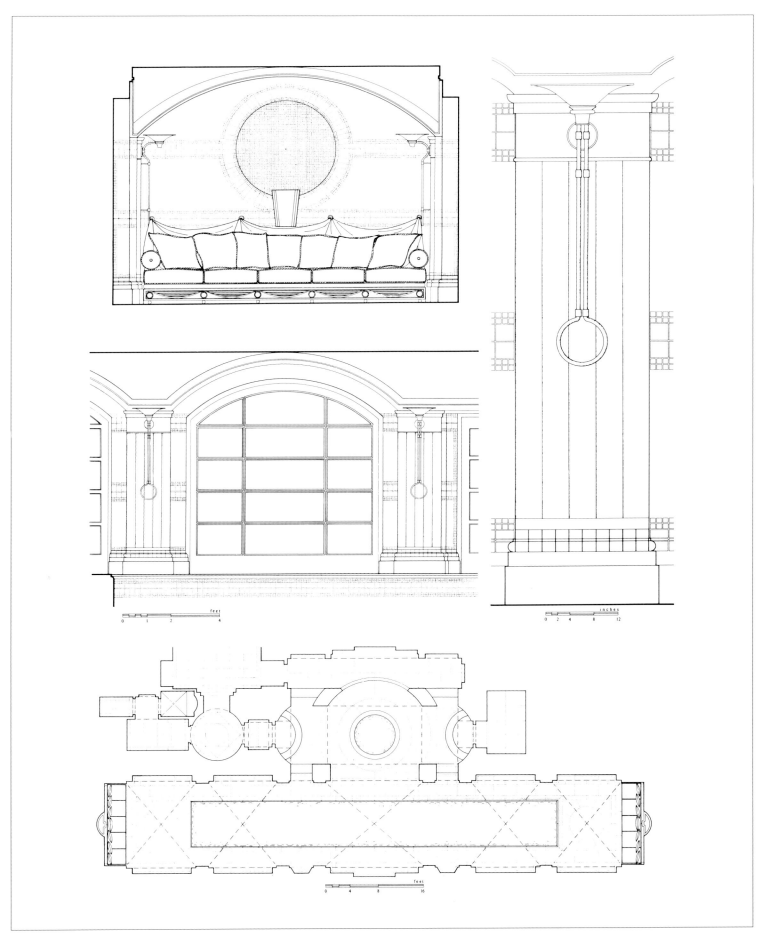

ABOVE AND CENTRE: DETAILS OF POOLROOM; *BELOW*: PLAN OF POOLROOM

RESIDENCE AT CALF CREEK
WATER MILL, NEW YORK, 1984-87

Located along a tributary of Mecox Bay, this house consciously works within the tradition of domestic resort architecture of eastern Long Island. The picturesque massing of gambrel roof, dormer windows, and projecting bays is used in combination with more formal Classical elements including a stylobate, Tuscan columns, and full entablatures. Raised above the ground on a rose-red brick base, the house has a traditional material palette of weathered red cedar shingles and white-painted wood trim.

Entry is through a vaulted porch, asymmetrically located in the east elevation which leads into a double-height stair hall. The plan is organised so that the more enclosed service areas are placed along the entrance facade, allowing the more formal rooms to be situated facing the view. Columns and shingled corner piers supporting the paired gambrels of the second floor at the water elevation recompose the asymmetry of the ground-floor plan while providing a large covered porch off the dining room.

Rising at the south-west corner of the house is a tower reminiscent of a shingled lighthouse. In its base is an octagonal study indirectly lit through an oculus, while at the second floor, a winding stair from a bedroom leads up to a playroom with a view of the bay and the ocean beyond.

OPPOSITE: VIEW OF MAIN ENTRANCE; *ABOVE*: VIEW FROM SOUTHWEST; *BELOW L TO R*: WEST ELEVATION, EAST ELEVATION

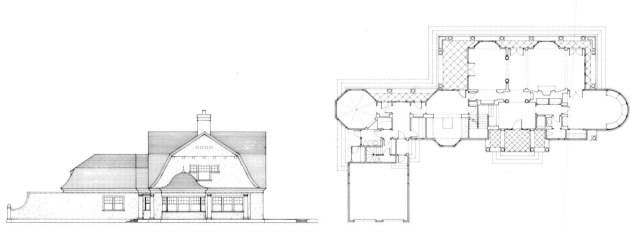

ABOVE: VIEW FROM NORTHWEST; *BELOW L TO R*: NORTH ELEVATION, FIRST FLOOR PLAN

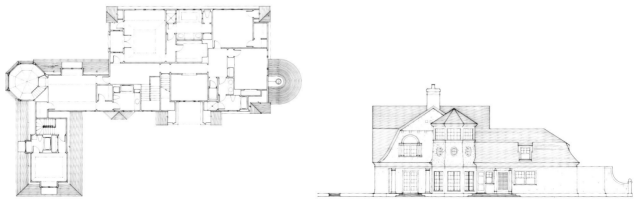

ABOVE: VIEW OF HOUSE AND POOL FROM SOUTH; *BELOW L TO R*: SECOND FLOOR PLAN, SOUTH ELEVATION

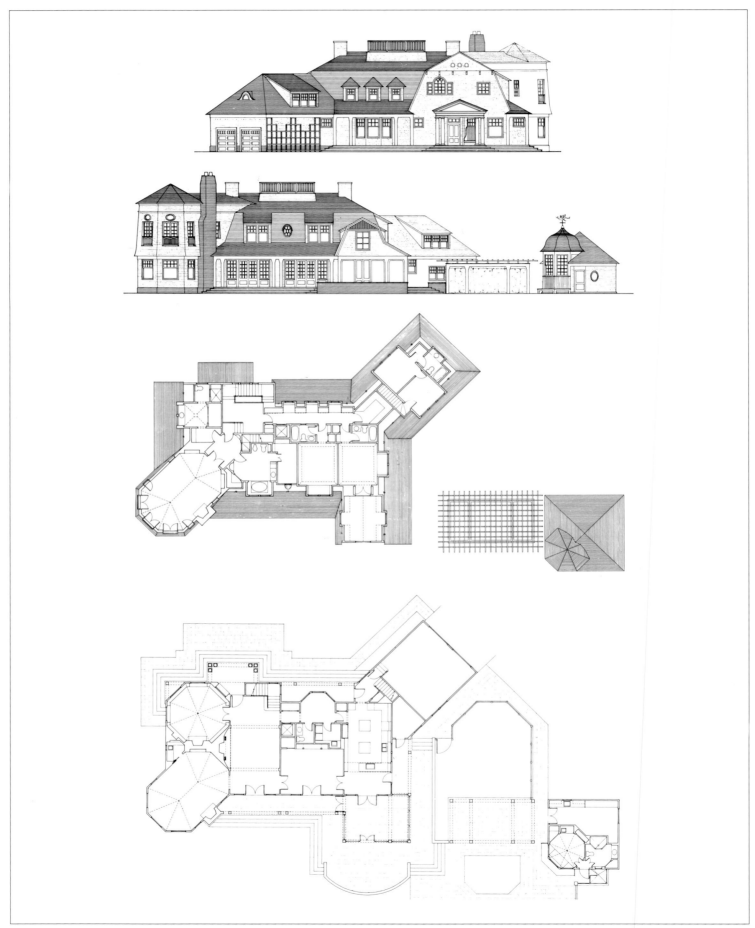

TOP TO BOTTOM: NORTHWEST ELEVATION, SOUTHEAST ELEVATION, SECOND FLOOR PLAN, FIRST FLOOR PLAN

SUNSTONE
QUOGUE, NEW YORK, 1984-87

The two-storey lighthouse-like tower at the southwest corner of the house offers a panoramic view of Shinnecock Bay from the living room and master bedroom within, and commands this four-acre peninsula without. From the widow's walk on the roof, the owner will survey the ocean beyond the barrier sandbar. The large gambrelled roof sweeps down over the verandas which encircle the house and affords the interior rooms comforting shade from the summer sun. The main roof is punctuated by a variety of dormer types and engages the smaller, subordinate garage and screened-porch roofs. The entry facade combines the vernacular gambrel with the Classical entry portico and Palladian stair-hall window.

Inside the entry hall is the centre of the first floor: it leads to the reception room, library, living and dining rooms and staircase to the second floor. Upstairs, the master bedroom suite is raised above the rest of the second floor to enhance the view from these rooms and allow for a raised faceted ceiling to the living room and library below. Open balconies surround the end of the master bedroom and serve as a lookout to the boats passing in the bay.

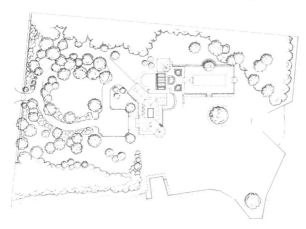

ABOVE: VIEW FROM SOUTHEAST; *BELOW*: SITE PLAN

RESIDENCE
MARBLEHEAD, MASSACHUSETTS, 1984-87

Set on a steeply pitched site with northerly views towards the water, this house continues the architectural traditions refined in the stone and timber cottages that dotted Boston's North Shore as well as the rest of coastal New England at the turn of the century. As the land falls away, the house's rubble stone foundation emerges, a high base anchoring the more finely detailed and picturesquely massed shingled superstructure. Responsive as it is to the delicate balance required between the requirements for good interior planning, solar orientation and view, the massing of the house –

replete with projecting bays and subsumed porches – is rendered sensible by a complex network of hipped roofs rising hierarchically to a unifying ridge line.

An L-shaped plan enhances the house's apparent compactness by lessening its perceived mass at the view side; at the front, this configuration defines an entry precinct separated by high garden walls from a service court. Within, planning centres around the planes and volumes of the cruciform living room, double-height entry hall and turreted stair to foster a relaxed interior consonant with the exterior's relative informality.

OPPOSITE: VIEW OF FRONT ENTRANCE; *ABOVE*: VIEW OF GARDEN AND HOUSE FROM NORTHEAST; *BELOW L TO R*: SECTION FACING SOUTHEAST, SECTION FACING SOUTHWEST

ABOVE: REAR VIEW OF HOUSE; *BELOW*: VIEW FROM NORTHWEST

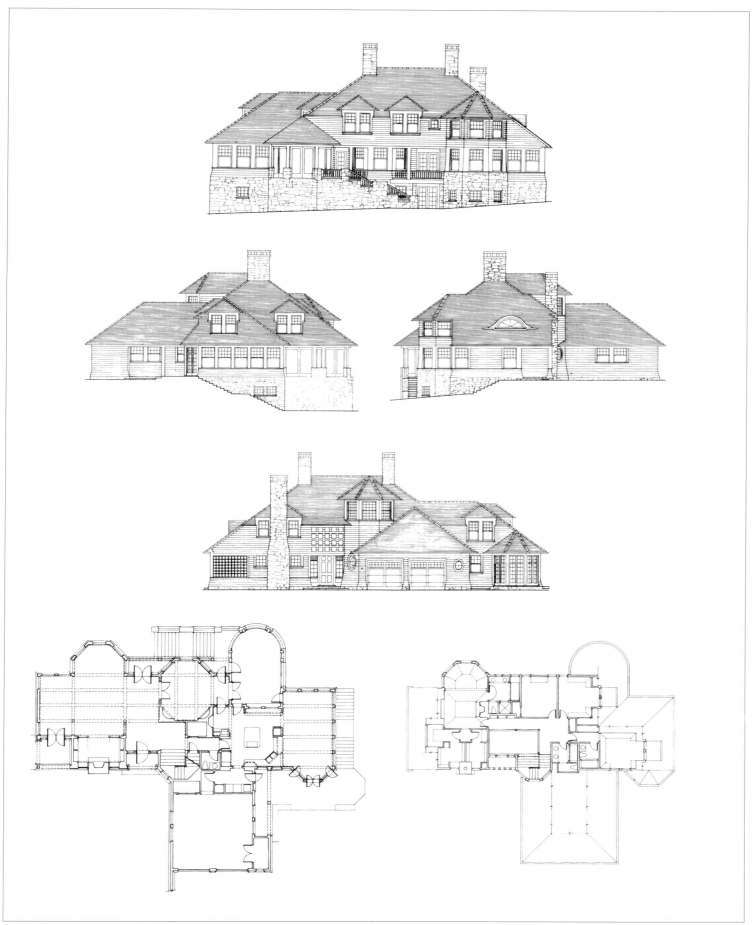

TOP TO BOTTOM L TO R: NORTHEAST ELEVATION; SOUTHEAST ELEVATION, NORTHWEST ELEVATION; SOUTHWEST ELEVATION; FIRST FLOOR PLAN, SECOND FLOOR PLAN

ABOVE: VIEW OF MAIN ENTRANCE; *BELOW*: VIEW OF HOUSE AND GARDEN FROM WEST

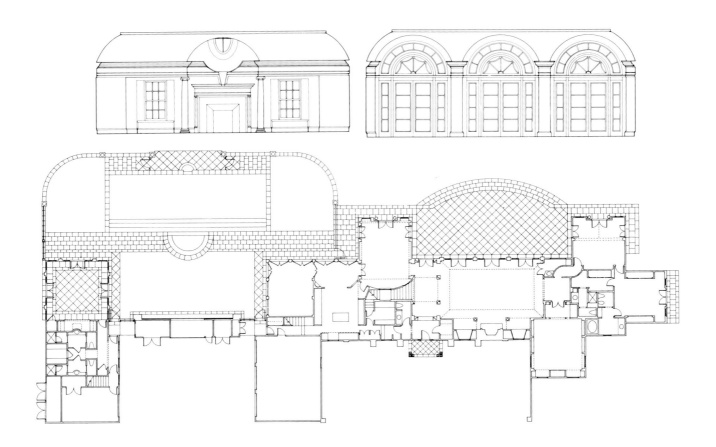

RESIDENCE
HEWLETT HARBOR, NEW YORK, 1984-88

This house addresses two very different contexts: the gently landscaped terrain of a golf course across the street in front, and a navigable channel that opens through the tidal marshes to Hewlett Bay at the back.

The entry court, a precisely formed exterior room, is the first in a series of spaces forming a sequence from the street to the water's edge. It is bounded by brick walls on two sides and on the third by the facade which takes cues from Sir John Soane's Pitzhanger Manor and from the Ashmolean Museum by CR Cockerell.

The unorthodox six-bay composition of the facade is intensified by the void frieze of the entablature above

the entry-porch roof which spills out from it, and the front door below. These elements, together with the delicately scaled colonnettes supporting a porch canopy, mediate between the public scale of the colossal Ionic order and the more intimate scale of the rooms within.

Beyond the facade, the proportions of the Ionic order and the order itself are used to create a series of rooms where the scale and detail of Classicism articulate the spatial interplay of a modern house. The principal rooms open, through French doors, to a terrace which wraps around the west side of the house, creating a plinth and extending the rooms toward the water.

TOP TO BOTTOM: LIVING ROOM EAST AND WEST ELEVATION, FIRST FLOOR PLAN, EAST ELEVATION, WEST ELEVATION

ABOVE: VIEW OF LIBRARY; *BELOW*: VIEW OF DRAWING ROOM

ROBERT AM STERN ARCHITECTS OFFICES
NEW YORK, NEW YORK, 1985

This 14-feet-high loft space is enclosed on three sides by a large band of industrial sash providing sweeping views of the Hudson River.

A principal axis of movement was created connecting Classically detailed rooms forming a sequence that is a double metaphor: in part for a house, in part for the design process as we pursue it. The reception and exhibition area leads into a library – the heart of the plan as it is of our design approach – and to the Principal's office which, with its views out to the city and river is a kind of urban garden where new buildings are germinated.

In order to heighten the contrast between the existing fabric and the architect's interventions, the window walls and ceiling of the warehouse were not repainted, leaving two open studio spaces, presided over by super-scale 'table' lamps in the Doric order that provide ambient illumination.

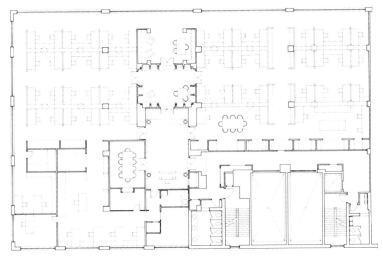

ABOVE: VIEW OF OF RECEPTION AND EXHIBITION AREA; *BELOW:* FLOOR PLAN

INTERNATIONAL HEADQUARTERS, MEXX INTERNATIONAL, BV
VOORSCHOTEN, THE NETHERLANDS, 1985-87

This corporate headquarters consists of an existing 25,000 square-feet, mid 19th-century silver factory renovated to accommodate executive offices on the ground floor and fashion design studios in what were the second-floor silversmiths' studios. Behind the existing structure a new, 25,000 square-feet addition provides fashion display areas, meeting rooms and further office space. Together the old and new buildings surround three sides of a double height, south-facing atrium and a reflecting pool.

The design strategy attempts to create a retrospective history for the entire building, as if it had grown over time from the reserved Baroque Classicism of the original facility to the freewheeling shapes of the addition that evoke the lighthearted and idiosyncratic spirit of Dutch Modernism.

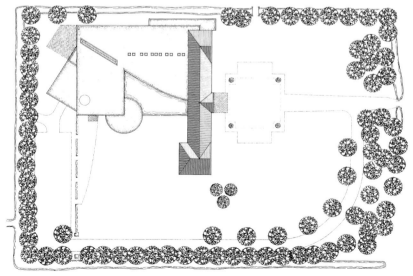

OPPOSITE: INTERIOR VIEW THROUGH CURTAIN WALL; *ABOVE*: NIGHT VIEW FROM SOUTH; *BELOW*: SITE PLAN

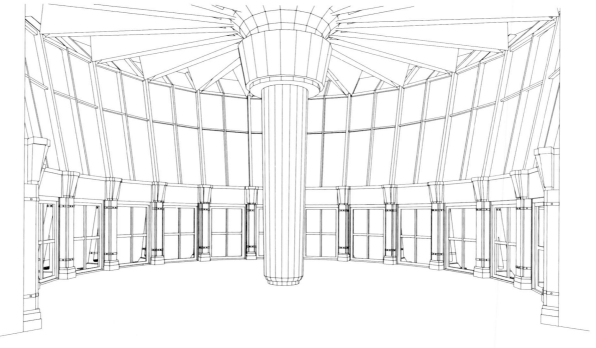

ABOVE: INTERIOR VIEW OF RESTAURANT; *BELOW*: AXONOMETRIC OF RESTAURANT

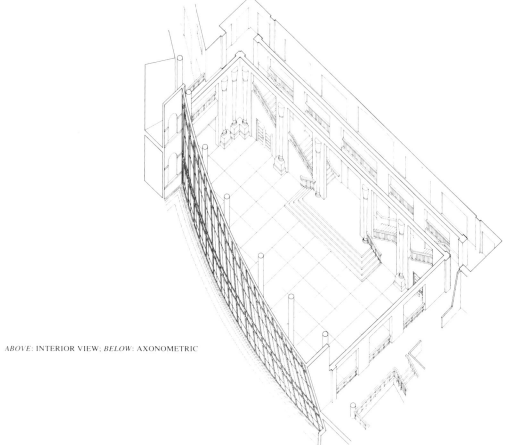

ABOVE: INTERIOR VIEW; *BELOW*: AXONOMETRIC

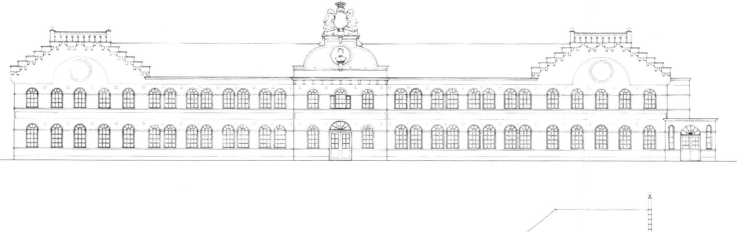

ABOVE: VIEW FROM SOUTHEAST; *CENTRE*: EAST ELEVATION; *BELOW*: SOUTH ELEVATION

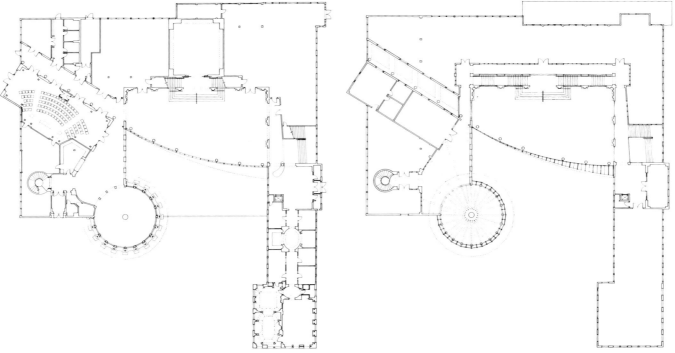

ABOVE: VIEW OF CURTAIN WALL AND REFLECTING POOL; *BELOW L TO R*: GROUND FLOOR PLAN, SECOND FLOOR PLAN

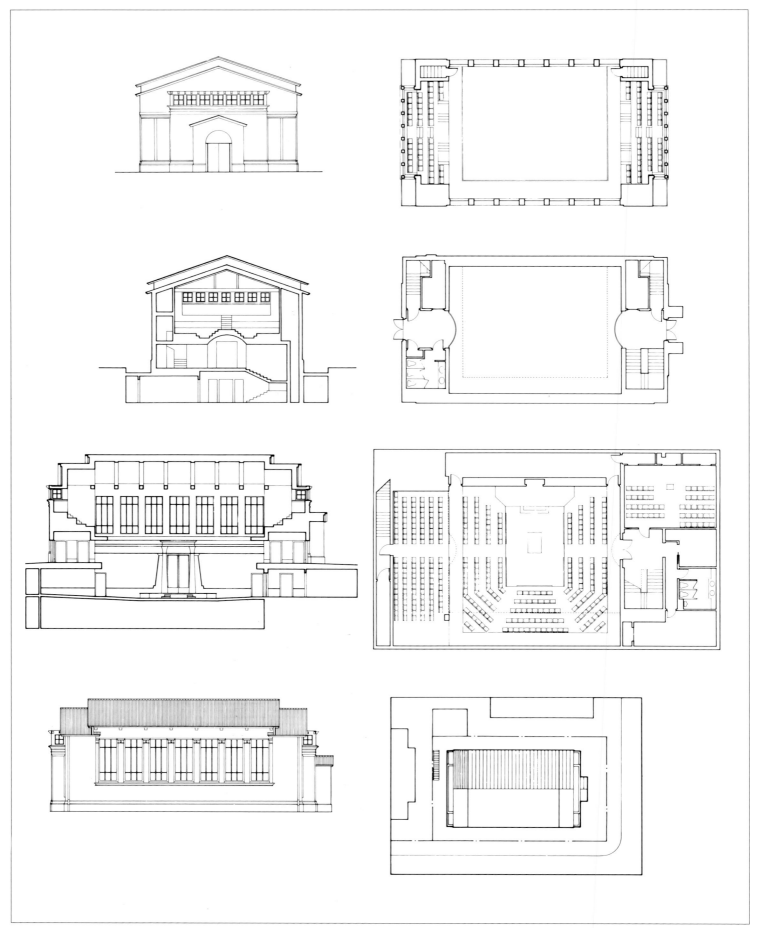

TOP TO BOTTOM: SOUTH ELEVATION, MEZZANINE PLAN; TRANSVERSE SECTION, ENTRY LEVEL PLAN; LONGITUDINAL SECTION, CONGREGATION PLAN; EAST ELEVATION, SITE PLAN

KOL ISRAEL CONGREGATION
BROOKLYN, NEW YORK, 1985-89

This synagogue for a growing congregation occupies a corner site in an established residential neighbourhood. To compliment the watery Mediterraneanism of the surrounding houses, the synagogue walls were built of red brick and stone, with a sheltered red tile roof.

Stringent setback and height limitations led to an unusual arrangement whereby the site was excavated to 10 feet, six inches below ground level, creating the largest possible area for the main sanctuary that rises past the entry level and balconies to a height of 34 feet.

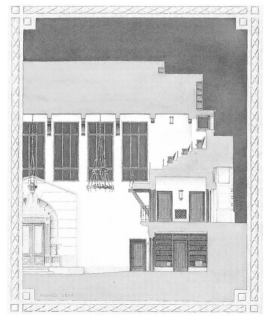

ABOVE: VIEW FROM SOUTH; *BELOW L TO R*: SECTIONAL DRAWING, DETAILS OF DECORATIVE AND BUILDING MATERIALS

ABOVE: VIEW UP RUSSIAN HILL FROM EAST; *BELOW*: NORTHWEST CORNER OF HOUSE

RESIDENCE ON RUSSIAN HILL
SAN FRANCISCO, CALIFORNIA, 1985-89

This extensive reconstruction and expansion of one of the oldest houses on Russian Hill consists of two significant compositional moves: a picturesque tower located asymmetrically at the north-west corner, where it forms a dramatic entry, and a straight run of stairs that cuts across the building to lead visitors to the principal living rooms which are located on the top floor affording spectacular views of the San Francisco Bay Area. Although the austere shingled idiom of the original house is retained in this reconstruction, with few clues given to the intricate play of planes and volumes that occur on the interior, the prominent corner tower clearly announces the reinvigorating transformation of the original house.

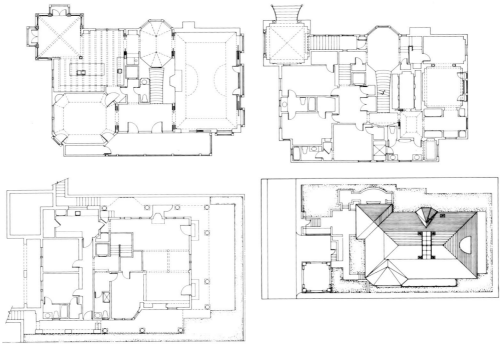

TOP TO BOTTOM L TO R: WEST AND EAST ELEVATIONS; SOUTH AND NORTH ELEVATIONS; THIRD AND SECOND FLOOR PLANS; FIRST FLOOR PLAN AND SITE PLAN

TEGELER HAFEN
BERLIN, GERMANY, 1985-89

This urban villa is one component in the reconstruction of Tegel, a suburb of Berlin ravaged by the war and hapless post-war planning. The master plan, prepared by Moore, Ruble, Yudell in 1980, calls for the creation of three distinct areas for housing, leisure and culture. Within the housing district, a five-storey serpentine range of row houses provides the background for six free-standing urban villas. A strict set of design guidelines was established by Charles Moore and his partners and by the German building code. One of these villas is the work of Moore; the others were by Stanley Tigerman, Paolo Portoghesi, Antoine Grumbach, and John Hejduk.

In an effort to break with the stark impersonality of most contemporary German social housing, our solution recalls the villas of the lakeside summer community of 19th-century Tegel, as well as the cool Classicism of Bruno Paul. Traditional gambrelled metal roofs, wrought-iron railings, and stucco walls with ceramic tile decoration are composed in symmetrical elevations. In plan, the three-storey villa arranges two one-bedroom and four two-bedroom units around a shared, daylit stair. All units have a double or triple exposure and an outdoor terrace or balcony. The unit plans balance the desire for a light, open plan and the need for privacy. Parking and individual storage lockers are located beneath the villa.

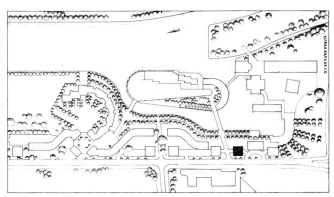

OPPOSITE: SOUTHEAST CORNER OF VILLA; *ABOVE:* GENERAL VIEW OF HOUSING DISTRICT; *BELOW:* SITE PLAN

ABOVE: VIEW FROM NORTH; *CENTRE L TO R*: NORTH ELEVATION, WEST ELEVATION; *BELOW L TO R*: SECOND FLOOR PLAN, ROOF GALLERY PLAN

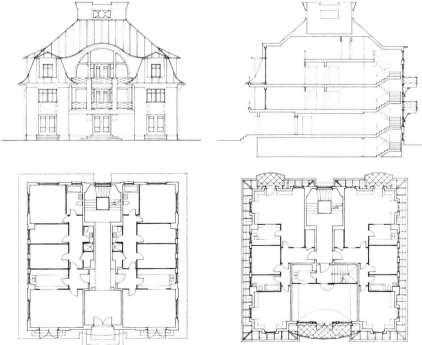

ABOVE: VIEW FROM SOUTH; *CENTRE L TO R*: SOUTH ELEVATION, SECTION LOOKING WEST; *BELOW L TO R*: GROUND FLOOR PLAN, THIRD FLOOR PLAN

ABOVE: INTERIOR VIEW OF DANCE STUDIO; *BELOW*: NIGHT VIEW FROM NORTHWEST

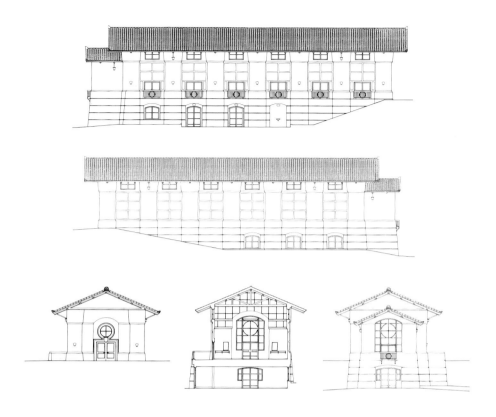

MASTER PLAN AND FINE ARTS STUDIO IV
FINE ARTS VILLAGE, UNIVERSITY OF CALIFORNIA, IRVINE, 1986-89

The master plan is intended to guide the expansion of the University's Fine Arts Complex through to the year 2010. Studio IV, an Art Studio, Dance and Drama Rehearsal Facility represents the first phase of that long term plan to be realised.

The master plan not only deals with issues of programme and growth, but also calls for a new vocabulary using red tile roofs, arcades, and naturally ventilated spaces in an effort to counterbalance the aesthetically and environmentally miscast negatives that constitute the first building of the arts village. Studio IV

transforms what was the back of the Fine Arts Village into a new front door, facing a major campus access road to the north and the recently completed University Events Center. The building creates a new south-facing plaza which serves as a 'Commons' for art students.

Using light frame and industrial building techniques the structure provides maximum open loft space within a limited budget. A design studio and slide library at the lower level open directly to a lawn which doubles as an outdoor amphitheatre. Two large rehearsal halls above open on to a covered south-facing terrace.

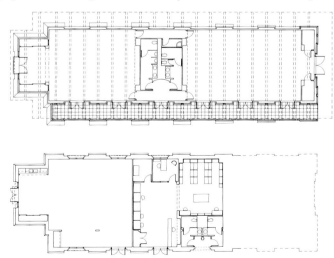

TOP TO BOTTOM L TO R: SOUTH ELEVATION, NORTH ELEVATION; EAST ELEVATION, SECTION THROUGH DANCE STUDIO, WEST ELEVATION; MAIN LEVEL PLAN, LOWER LEVEL PLAN

ABOVE: VIEW OF FOUNTAIN AND COURTYARD HOUSES; *BELOW*: REAR VIEW OF HOUSING COMPLEX

GRAND HARBOR
VERO BEACH, FLORIDA, 1986-89

Set on the Indian River, Grand Harbor is a resort community built around two golf courses and a marina. Our office was responsible for the unrealised Harbor Center which was to include 90,000 square-feet of retail space with 116 residential units above, and a separate complex, Wood Duck Island, where 67 townhouses were built, but three clubhouses were not.

The Harbor Center incorporated shops, restaurants and a market to serve not only the Grand Harbor community but also residents in the greater Vero Beach area as well as tourists. Stucco walls, clay tile roofs and

shutters, arcades and small courts, evoked the Mediterraneanism of Addison Mizner's Worth Avenue. Apartments above the retail space promoted a planning ideal: a village centre rather than a shopping mall.

The clubs and townhouses of Wood Duck Island were designed to work together as a cohesive urban unit with a hierarchy of streets and paths, landscaped walls and intimate courts. The clubs were grouped to create a formal plaza, providing the gateway from which a grand boulevard led to the villas which, in turn, were arranged around small courtyards.

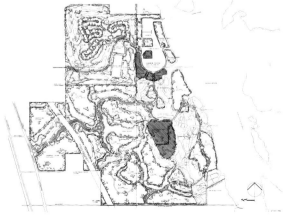

ABOVE: AERIAL VIEW OF 'PARCEL P' HOUSING COMPLEX; *BELOW*: OVERALL PLAN OF DEVELOPMENT

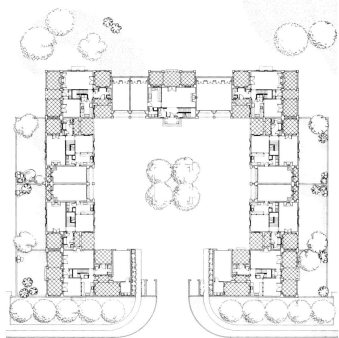

ABOVE: VIEW OF HOUSING FROM VERANDA; *BELOW*: COURTYARD HOUSING, FIRST FLOOR PLANS

ABOVE: VIEW FROM WITHIN HOUSING COURTYARD; *BELOW*: AXONOMETRIC OF COURTYARD HOUSES

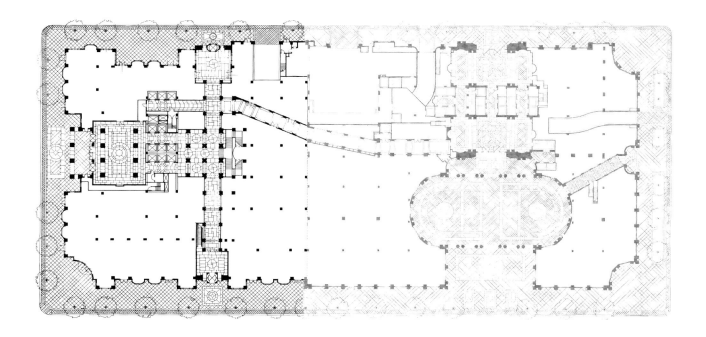

TWO TWENTY TWO BERKELEY STREET
BOSTON, MASSACHUSETTS, 1986-91

A mixed-use building in Boston's Back Bay combining offices, shops, a winter garden, and 400 cars parked underground, 222 Berkeley Street is the second phase of a controversial retail-office complex in one of America's most architecturally elaborate urban centres.

The familiar Boston palette of red brick, granite and limestone has been adapted to a complexly massed office tower, shaped in response to the different urban pressures on each of its sides, and resolved in a pavilion-like crown to create a distinctive skyline silhouette that places our design firmly within the American tradition of Classical skyscrapers.

The main lobby, reached through a severely Classical portico facing Berkeley Street, leads past the office lobby to monumental stairs rising to the second-storey winter garden, a top lit, five-storey high room that functions as light court and public gathering place. A continuous row of shops faces Boylston Street, interrupted at one point by an entrance leading to the north-south mid-block pedestrian arcade. To emphasise the public nature of the arcade and the winter garden it leads to, the Boylston Street entrance is flanked by paired Ionic columns carrying urns and entered through a revolving door housed in a tempietto.

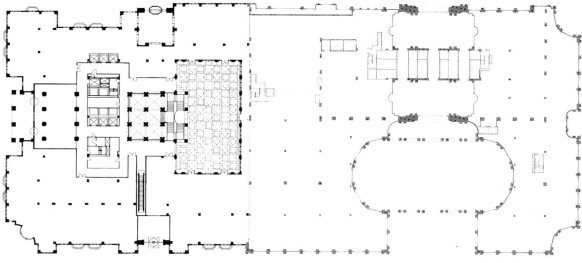

OPPOSITE: PHOTOMONTAGE FROM BERKELEY ST; *ABOVE*: GROUND FLOOR PLAN; *BELOW*: SECOND FLOOR PLAN

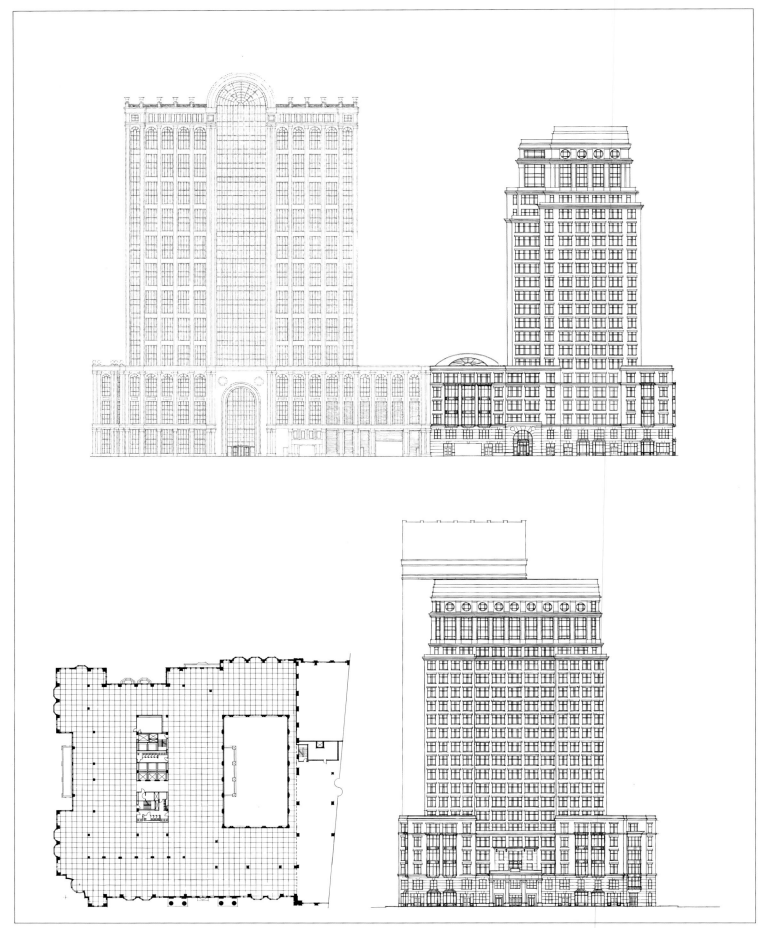

ABOVE: ST JAMES AVENUE ELEVATION *BELOW L TO R*: PLAN OF FLOORS THREE TO FIVE, BERKELEY ST ELEVATION

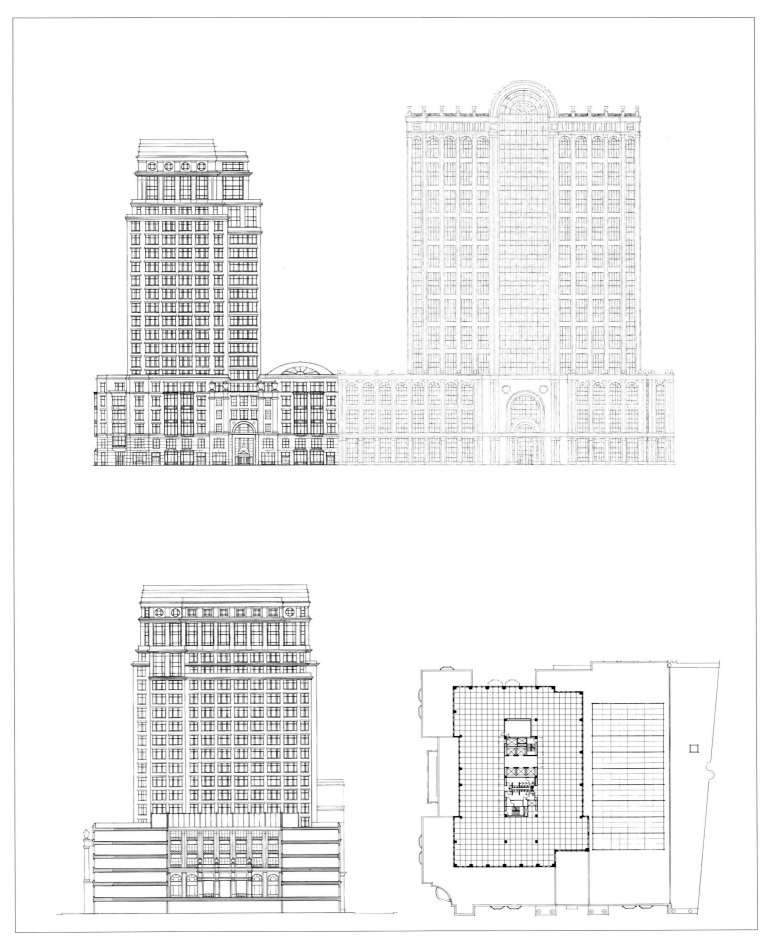

ABOVE: BOYLSTON ST ELEVATION; *BELOW L TO R*: BUILDING CROSS SECTION, PLAN OF FLOORS SEVEN TO SEVENTEEN

CASTING CENTER, WALT DISNEY WORLD
LAKE BUENA VISTA, FLORIDA, 1987-89

The Casting Center faces Interstate 4, but is entered from Buena Vista Drive within Walt Disney World proper. The building is the sole representation of the Disney company on the Interstate, and is intended not only to house personnel functions, but also to convey the company spirit to prospective employees, housing the central hiring facility, the Employee Relations Division and Labour Relations Department. The building is organised as two block-like abutments and a bridge spanning a marsh. The southern end of the bridge houses the entrance rotunda; the northern end, the General Employment Lobby.

Inside and out, the building's imagery reinterprets themes to be found in Disney's movies and theme parks: campanile-like skylights, turrets, futuristic airfoil shapes and elaborately tiled surfaces as well as Mickey Mouse water scuppers. Visitors enter under the airfoil canopy,

open bronze doors by grasping door pulls modelled on characters from Alice in Wonderland, *and begin new journeys to employment, a processional sequence of spaces that start in an oval rotunda adorned with 12 gilt statues of Disney's most illustrious characters. Continuing along a 150 feet long skylit ramp lined with* trompe l'oeil *panels that offer highly interpretive views of Disney World as well as the roadside context, the job seeker is introduced to the heart of the building without violating the privacy of workers who occupy the two floors of offices. The ramp is not only a way to effectively handle the large crowds of job seekers but also a surrogate for the visitors' experience in the Disney parks, where ramps are used to channel crowds and heighten the sense of expectation for individual attractions. The trip up the ramp culminates in the General Employment Lobby, under the second campanile.*

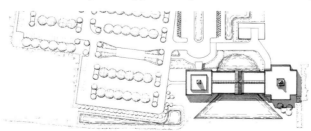

OPPOSITE: NIGHT VIEW OF AIRFOIL ENTRANCE CANOPY; *ABOVE*: VIEW FROM INTERSTATE 4; *BELOW*: SITE PLAN

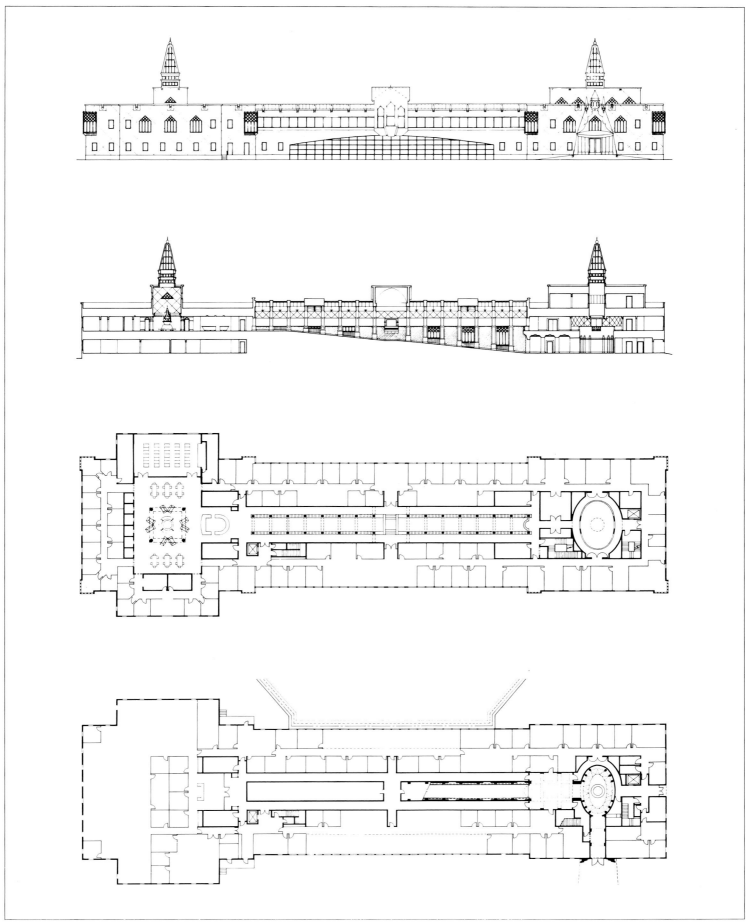

OPPOSITE: CORNER DETAIL; *TOP TO BOTTOM*: WEST ELEVATION, LONGITUDINAL SECTION, SECOND FLOOR PLAN, FIRST FLOOR PLAN

OPPOSITE: INTERIOR VIEW OF ENTRANCE ROTUNDA; *ABOVE*: SECTION THROUGH RAMP; *BELOW*: SECTION THROUGH LOBBY

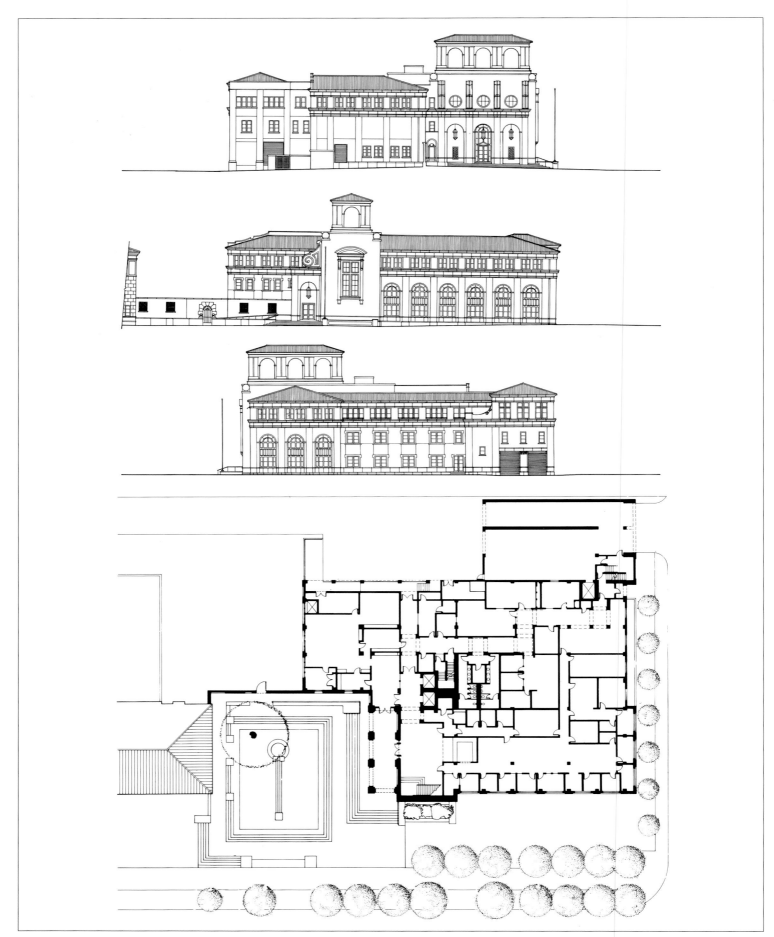

TOP TO BOTTOM: SOUTH ELEVATION, EAST ELEVATION, NORTH ELEVATION, GROUND FLOOR PLAN

POLICE BUILDING
PASADENA, CALIFORNIA, 1987-90

The first major addition to Pasadena's Civic Center in 20 years, the Police Building, occupying a subordinate position in relation to the landmark City Hall (John Bakewell, Jr & Arthur Brown, Jr, 1925-1927), Public Library (Myron Hunt & HC Chambers, 1927) and Civic Auditorium (Bergstrom, Bennett & Haskell, 1932), has as its focal point a tower capped by an open-air structure, recalling the colossal open-air dome of City Hall. Located asymmetrically, this tower is visually

buttressed by a two-storey arcaded porch supporting scrolled volutes. The porch, which helps enclose a courtyard and is related in scale to the adjacent Southern California Gas Building (architect unknown, 1924) leads to a three-storey entrance lobby. In a situation where issues of security are paramount, the appearance of an armed fortress is carefully avoided – the Police Building expresses civic grandeur while maintaining a welcoming, public image.

ABOVE L TO R: VIEW OF LOBBY, DETAIL OF ENTRANCE PORCH: *BELOW:* VIEW FROM SOUTHEAST

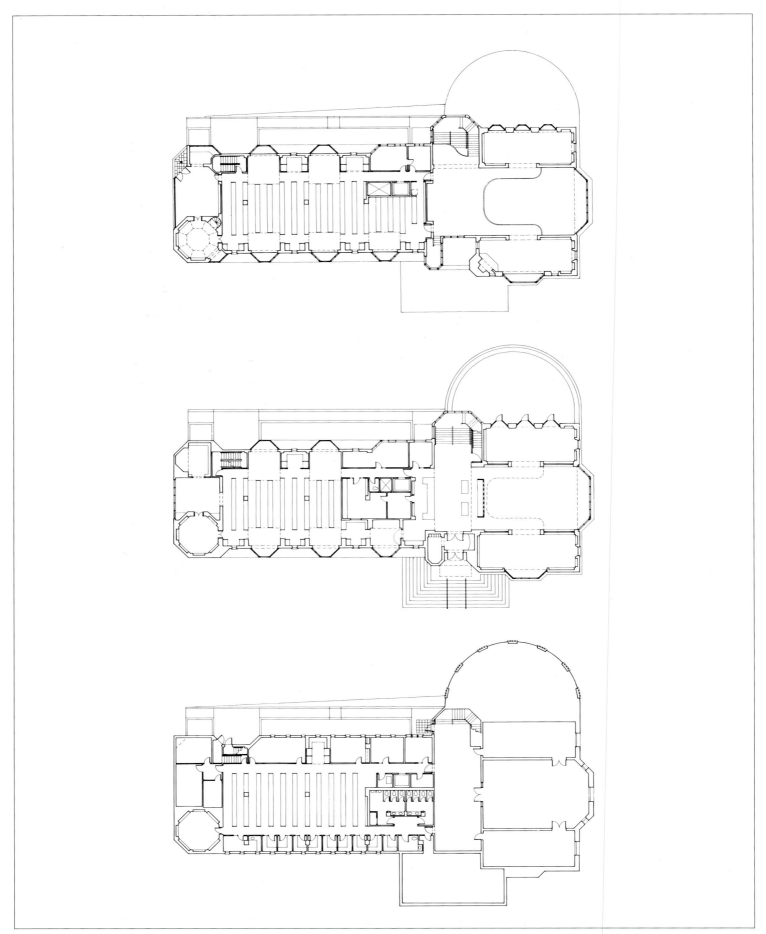

ABOVE: UPPER FLOOR PLAN; *CENTRE*: MAIN FLOOR PLAN; *BELOW*: LOWER FLOOR PLAN

OHRSTROM LIBRARY, ST PAUL'S SCHOOL
CONCORD, NEW HAMPSHIRE, 1987-91

Located at the centre of the village-like campus of this traditional New England boarding school, the Ohrstrom Library forms the boundary wall for two quadrangles: to the south, it joins a residential group to create an intimate courtyard; to the north it forms the fourth wall of a larger space that is both the symbolic and actual centre of the campus, counterpointing in a dialogue across time and space, the school's original chapel (1859), and Henry Vaughan's masterly essay in the Gothic, the chapel of St Peter and St Paul (1888).

The principal point of reference for the library design was James Gamble Rogers' School House (1937) built

at a little remove from the centre. Rogers' building inspired the red brick and Briraar Hill stone facades of our design as well as the character of the oak panelling used on the interior.

On the inside the library combines the most up to date information retrieval technology with traditional reading rooms and more intimately scaled niches that combine quiet individual study with easy access to bookstacks. The nave-like plan is entered at the crossing which separates the stacks from the specialised reading rooms, gathered around a two-storey-high vaulted room that opens to a view of Lower School Pond.

ABOVE: VIEW FROM THE NORTH; *BELOW*: INTERIOR VIEW OF MAIN FLOOR

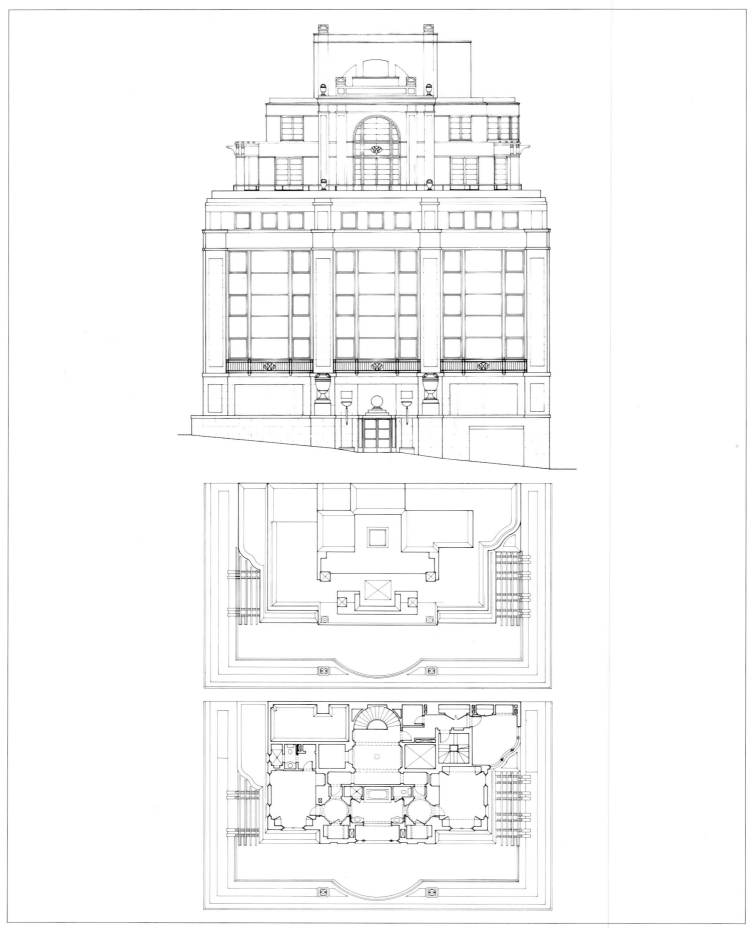

TOP TO BOTTOM: WEST ELEVATION, ROOF PLAN, SEVENTH FLOOR PLAN

BANCHO HOUSE
TOKYO, JAPAN, 1988-89

Bancho House, a five-storey office building surmounted by a two-storey penthouse, overlooks the British Embassy. From its top floors there are sweeping views of the Imperial Palace Gardens and the skyline of the Marunouchi district, Tokyo's principal business centre.

Sheathed in flamed Absolute Black granite and honed Atlantic Green granite, stainless steel finished aluminium, and grey-tinted glass, Bancho House synthe-

sises modern elements and traditional Classicism as a gesture to the architecture of the 70-year-old British Embassy and also to the client's preference for traditional Western architecture.

The principal rooms of the penthouse open out onto a rooftop terrace that is framed by pergolas at either end which shelter it from neighbours and emphasise the dramatic view to the south east.

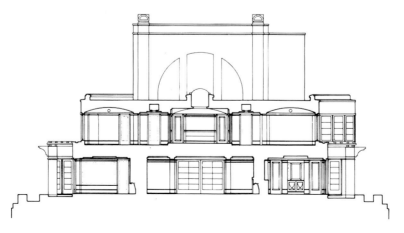

ABOVE L TO R: CORNER VIEW, REAR VIEW; *BELOW*: SECTION

TWO VENTURE PLAZA, IRVINE CENTER
IRVINE, CALIFORNIA, 1988-90

This 100,000 square feet, five-storey office building is located in an office park at the confluence of two of Southern California's busiest freeways. Within the office park it occupies a pivotal corner site, but access to the building is possible only through an interior cul de sac. The building is sited diagonally to the corner to heighten its impact and to address the entry drive which slices diagonally across the square site from the cul de sac. Twin parking structures flank the entry drive helping to reinforce the approach axis leading to the entry court.

In a bid to be sympathetic to the Southern California developer tradition yet distinct and self assured, the

imagery and detailing of the building is sleek and taut, while steadfastly Classical in its composition.

A symmetrical five-storey block with short wings which pull forward to help further define the entry court, is announced by a two-storey free-standing porch, supported by four truncated obelisks capped by shallow metal urns. The building is clad in cast panels that mimic Roman travertine with silver-like aluminium window frames and window returns. Balconies at the fifth floor, appropriate for the mild Southern California climate, together with the broad projecting silver metal visor, provide a strong skyline silhouette.

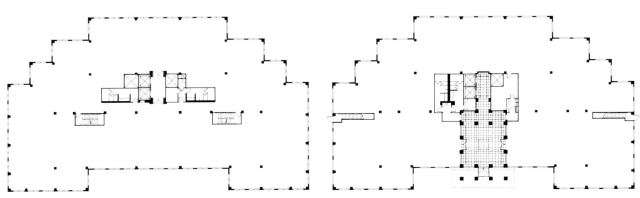

OPPOSITE: DETAIL OF ENTRANCE FACADE; *ABOVE*: VIEW OF FRONT; *BELOW L TO R*: TYPICAL FLOOR PLAN, FIRST FLOOR PLAN

TEGELER HAFEN, BERLIN, GERMANY, 1985-89

BEGINNINGS

'Chance favours the prepared mind'. (Louis Pasteur)

Evelyn Waugh has observed that innovation in art is usually a kind of revivalism, in which an appeal to an earlier and purer virtue challenges a debased conception of the immediate past.[1] This is surely true for me; the architecture that years ago I believed I would myself one day design was wholly in disrepute when I began to practise, and only now am I beginning to rediscover its traditions in my own work and that of others.

An artist cannot choose his themes; they become his by virtue of what he knows and feels. In a curious way mine were chosen for me before my formal education in design began. I had grown up as much on the proto-Modernist architecture which Hitchcock labelled a 'New Tradition' as on the early work of Le Corbusier, Mendelsohn or Mies, and had grown up within an urban context that can best be described as metropolitan in its scale, sophistication and complexity. I have only recently come to realise that much said to me later by teachers and fellow students about what architecture was and should be, ignored or disparaged what I admired, and tended to sever me from the roots of my early experience. As I studied architecture, the lessons implicit in the buildings and places I had grown up with were virtually disregarded by most of my teachers and my fellow students. For many of the former, the frame of reference was Gropius' Cambridge and Mies' Chicago, not Le Corbusier's Paris or Raymond Hood's New York. I was surprised by this, but, equally intent on learning the craft of architecture, I discarded the earlier part of my architectural experience as I set out to become a 'modern' architect.

This process of disorientation is easily explained. When I began to be conscious of architecture I was able not only to see everywhere about me distinguished examples of the 'New Tradition', but also to learn about this kind of architecture when I consulted library books on 'modern' or 'contemporary' architecture: Hugh Ferris, Charles Harris Whitaker, Thomas Talmage, FR Yerbury and Sheldon Cheney were my early *Cicerone*. Only later did I become conscious of the so-called mainstream of Modernism through exhibits at the Museum of Modern Art and the creamy paper of Giedion's beguiling books. Only then was it suggested to me that Mendelsohn (whom I admired extravagantly) was somehow vulgar; that Rob Mallet-Stevens was not serious and Willem Dudok was not really a very good architect at all (though Bijvoet and Duiker were masters of incontrovertible integrity and innovation!). Nevertheless, by the time I read Giedion's *Space, Time and Architecture* I had been so involved with messages other than the high-Modernist polemic (twice already had I read Hitchcock's *Modern Architecture* of 1929), that I never absorbed that polemic into my system as whole-heartedly as others of my generation and the one behind me seem to have. In seeking to resolve the seeming contradictions of all this, I was helped by two great teachers: Everard M Upjohn at Columbia, who taught me about the 'Elements of Architecture' in a way that avoided but did not disparage the Modernist movement, and Vincent Scully, at Yale, who made it absolutely clear that the history of modern architecture was much broader, far more complex and much more culturally engaged than Giedion's canonical mainstream lead one to believe. In fact, I only chose to study architecture at Yale because I was persuaded by a friend, Stephen Baldwin, that Paul Rudolph was a brilliant design critic – which he was – and because

Vincent Scully and Carroll Meeks were there. I had read their books and thought them far and away the most sympathetic discussions of the recent past available.

On reflection, it does not seem very surprising that I chose to write about George Howe when I was at Yale, despite the fact that virtually no one on the faculty who had known him held him in particularly high esteem either as a person or as an architect. Howe fascinated me because his life and career reflected the shift in values (or was it merely a change of style?) that I found so confounding in my own very limited experience. And while in my work as a novice designer in the 1960s I couldn't even begin to imagine a way to express my unease and sense of loss which this shift had brought about, I could do so in a book. In the 1960s and early 1970s I believed myself a modern architect, yet not a contemporary one. Excepting the work of Venturi and Moore, there was little in the current architectural scene that I felt good about. The complexities of the struggles of the 1920s fascinated me, but I could not overcome a sense that the 'battle of the moderns' – that is the battle between the progressive and revolutionary styles – had drained architecture of its vitality and alienated it from its own traditions. I still believe myself a 'modern'; but only now, with the recuperation of earlier traditions taking place everywhere, is it possible for me to imagine myself a contemporary architect as well.

At the start of my architectual studies, the differences between progressive traditionalism and revolutionary Modernism seemed largely stylistic. A child of Gotham, I marvelled at the monuments of the 50s – Lever House, Manufacturers Hanover Bank, the UN, Seagram's – but equally loved Pennsylvania Station, the Chrysler Building (especially its lobby) and the towers of Wall Street (especially 55 Exchange Place). All were good architecture to me: I didn't consider the differences between so-called traditional and so-called modern building in ideological terms.

Many of my generation are not so fortunate as to be from a place; some grew up as petroleum-age pioneers, adrift in the amorphous suburbs of the post World War II era; many more never lived in one spot for long enough to have its special qualities sink in. As a New York City boy I have always felt rooted in this place. Henry James' speculations on the interaction between associational values and beloved places intrigue me. Moved by his visit to George Washington's house at Mount Vernon, James explored the role of association in the establishment of what he called 'The Sense of the Place':

> The Beauty of the site as we stand there, becomes but the final aspect of the man; under which everything conduces to a single great representative image, under which every feature of the scene, every object in the house, however trivial, borrows from it and profits by it.

James puts the problem succinctly:

> Association does, at Mount Vernon, simply what it likes with us – it is of so beautiful and noble a sort; and to this end it begins by making us unfit to say whether or not we would in its absence have noticed the house for any material grace at all.[2]

As a designer, I choose to interpret James' sense of place in the broadest possible way; hence the principles of contextual design which I first argued for in 1977.[3] Allusionism in art is a process of historical and cultural response in which the form of a work takes on characteristics of previous work. The sincerest form of allusionism may of course be imitation: not the simple-minded corruption of the copy or duplicate, but the carefully wrought variation on a known theme that Sir Joshua advocated in his *Discourses to the Students of the Royal Academy*. Reynolds wrote:

> It is indisputably evident that a great part of every man's life must be employed in collecting materials for the exercise of genius. Invention, strictly speaking, is little more than a new combination of those images which have been previously gathered and deposited in the memory; nothing can come of nothing: he who has laid up no materials can produce no combinations . . . imitation only, variety, and even originality of invention, is produced. What is learned from others becomes really our own, sinks deep, and is never forgotten, nay, it is by seizing on this clue that we proceed forward, and get further and further in enlarging the principle and improving the practice of our art. Study, therefore, the great works of the great masters forever. Study those masters . . . consider them as models which you are to imitate, and at the same time as rivals with whom you are to contend.[4]

To the extent that I am able, I seek to combine the lessons of Reynolds and of James. Until the Modernist break with tradition in the 1920s, such was always the case with architects – to look at what Edith Wharton has described as the 'custom of the country' and see how the best architects who worked in the area were able to raise that custom to the higher level of art. Despite the homogenisation of experience that industrialisation has brought about, a homogenisation that architects have for too long accepted as an unquestioned benefit (why is an International Style a good thing?) a number of places have been able to insulate themselves to a remarkable extent from disjunctive change: resort communities in the eastern United States, whole sections of major cities (eg New York, London, Paris, San Francisco, Rome). Such places pose a critical challenge for architecture in our time and make clear that we need to turn back the clock to the extent that we must reunite current production with the traditions that a previous generation worked so hard to subvert. In turning the clock back, however, we are not stopping it; rather we are giving it a chance to refresh itself and proceed with a full sense of its own possibilities, released from the trap of the perennial present. The New Tradition admired by Hitchcock represents a synthesis which architecture can still achieve.

To put this another way, I define 'modern' architecture in very broad terms. In my view I see Modernism from the 1920s to the 60s and the Post-Modernism of the present as phases of an on-going architectural culture extending back to the Renaissance.[5] In this broad continuum, which is in effect that of the Western Humanist Tradition, three expressive modes are evident: the Classical, the vernacular and the mechanical. The Modernism of the 20s to the 50s sought to transcend the first two through a hyper-emphasis on the third; Modernism's leading architects and ideologues regarding the machine as the inevitable victor in a positivistic race towards Utopia.

The lessons of modern architecture before the rise of Modernism abundantly suggest that the eclectic approach of the New Tradition had within it the capacity to suggest a workable design methodology for an architecture as culturally complex and inventive as the society which spawned it, yet legible to those who use it. To the architects of the pre-Modernist New Tradition, architecture was capable of high-blown rhetoric and everyday speech, new programmes and new materials were seen as stimulants for invention within traditional form languages rather than as sources of despair leading to their abandonment.

A methodology that embodies the interaction of the Classical,

the vernacular and the mechanical components of Modernism (a process of hybridisation reflecting careful assessment of the programme's socio-cultural and physically contextual conditions) can lead to an architecture whose meanings are more accessible to more people at various levels of understanding. Such a synthesis is not particularly new. It was, in fact, the normative condition of modern architecture in the pre-Modernist era and was articulated over 100 years ago by Thomas Hope. Hope advocated a stylistic eclecticism anchored to the present by virtue of the inherent materiality of architectural production, an eclecticism which would lead, he believed, to a modern architecture that could be described as 'Our Own'.[6] Such a synthesis can be seen in the work of HH Richardson, who combined his principal themes, the Romanesque for public and religious buildings and the American colonial for houses, with a Classical syntax absorbed while a student at the Ecole des Beaux Arts. Antonio Gaudí introduced representations of nature at a grand scale to the Parc Guell and raised such a synthesis to a high, as did Frank Lloyd Wright at the Imperial Hotel. Wright's hotel combines a Classical plan with an overall massing of clearly Florentine origins (compare the Pazzi chapel with the central pavilion of Wright's scheme), transformed by virtue of an amazing manipulation of local masonry techniques in combination with reinforced concrete and an equally amazing adaptation of American pre-Columbian decorative motifs to suggest a Japanese tradition of architectural embellishment that clearly never existed. What I am arguing for, and what these buildings exemplify, is an architectural culture in which buildings can be 'read', in which connections with forms from the past help to reaffirm a more normative role for architecture, not only in its relationship to the building task but also in its relationship to culture as a whole. Revolutionary Modernism has collapsed because it could neither posit a convincing way beyond the Western humanist tradition nor sustain the existing cultural condition in all its diversity.

In my early houses I strove to break with the conventionalised late Modernism of the 50s and 60s and to root the work in a contextually meaningful tradition. In this I usually relied on the palette of building materials used in traditional buildings to establish a continuity with the place. Yet seldom did I embrace the forms of the local tradition, preferring instead to attempt to devise new ones (that is, to innovate), struggling to be sympathetic to the place yet breaking the historical code in order to make the work 'original', 'modern' or 'interesting'. In this process of code-breaking, I actually denied my own natural instincts towards the introduction of representational elements taken from the stylistic and typological models which I was interested in emulating. I denied my own best instincts to do architecture as I knew it to be, in favour of doing it as I felt it 'ought' to be. I permitted myself to accept the argument that the constricting climate of our times requires expression in a diminished vocabulary of form and a reduced spirit, as reflected in the new work's attitude to the sense of the place.

Yet architecture is not an industrial process; it is a fine art. The economics of construction have changed radically and Western societies appear to have much less money available to build than they had 50 years ago – in fact, this gradual impoverishment of resources has run a steady course since the Renaissance. The modern era has been one of continually diminished expectations for architects. Consider how disappointed Palladio must have been confined as he was to a country house practice in a remote corner of the Italian peninsula while dreaming of temples on the Roman Forum. Yet how skilfully he forged a synthesis between his dreams and his circumstances in his bold combinations of house, temple and stoa – as at Maser, where he modelled an ordinary local building material (stucco) to evoke the glories of marble and other stones that had been the ancient Roman architect's stock-in-trade.

In our own time, even the construction of generously budgeted public buildings is afflicted by the absence of a positive sense of craft or the subtle vocabulary of detail which is its concomitant. The result is work only moderately more satisfying than the typical production of the market place. A comparison between John Russell Pope's and IM Pei's work at the National Gallery confirms this; the architecture of our time has been immeasurably diminished by imposing on itself restrictions concerning the sources of its forms, marrying given traditional materials to the techniques of engineering and serial production, rather than using machine-made materials to revivify ancient, familiar and refined old forms.

In the traditionally modern approach which I advocate, the building's overall shape is usually conventional; visual interest derives from the careful positioning and proportion of components and from the fineness of detail. Architecture need not be immediately shocking, and freshness need not mean strangeness. Clear, familiar shapes allow the viewer to immediately comprehend a building's function and intention. The 'big statement' once expected of architecture is, I feel, better deferred to particular conditions of site and programmatic circumstances. Yet concurrently a work should not communicate all of itself at once. The detail that distinguishes one building from the next, by playing a discrete and subtle variation on familiar themes, can produce a continually enriching experience, a nourishing dialogue between the work, the place and the viewer's personal body of images and associations.

Given the diversity inherent in this methodology, with its insistence on a direct response to particularities of place and programme, one might well ask what commonalities exist between individual buildings within an architect's *oeuvre* – or to put it more specifically, is the thread of intention the only one to establish a continuity and personality in the work of a particular architect and his atelier? Equally one can wonder whether such identification is particularly relevant, except to art historians. Certainly the houses my office has produced over the past ten years, though they do not have an immediately recognisable stamp of personal style, do cumulatively express the process of intellectual and emotional transformation, or maturation, which is the distinguishing mark of an individual's search for meaning. I merely state this dilemma; I have no easy answer. In fact, I increasingly believe there are none and that the real contributions one can make are not identical with issues of individual personal expression as many seem to believe. Moreover I know architecture is not an art of solitude and I wish to make clear that the cause of my development to date must surely be charted in relationship to that of my office. I hope I have influenced my collaborators; I know they have influenced me. For me, architecture is not a lonely process of self-revelation but a struggle to commemorate the place and the culture. Despite the chaos that rages everywhere around us, each building still presents an opportunity to affirm and re-establish the inherent order of things.

Notes

1 Mark Amory, ed, *The letters of Evelyn Waugh*, Ticknor & Fields, New York, 1980, p 215. This essay, 'Beginnings', was first published in *Architecture and Urbanism*, July 1982, Extra Edition, pp 13-16.

2 James, *American Scene*, Indiana University Press, Bloomington and London, 1968, pp 335-338.

3 See my 'At the Edge of Post-Modernism', *Architectural Design*, Vol 47, No 4, London, 1977, pp 275-286.

4 See Joshua Reynolds, *Discourses on Art*, ed Robert R Wark, New Haven, 1975, pp 27, 96, 113.

5 See my 'Doubles of Post-Modern', first published in *Harvard Architectural Review*, Vol 1, Spring, 1980.

6 Hope, *An Historical Essay on Architecture*, third edition, London, 1840, Vol I, p 492.

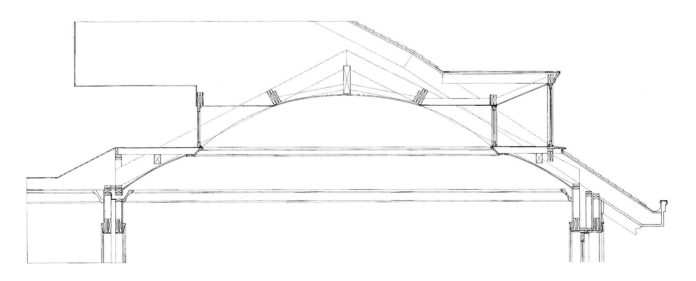

ABOVE: RESIDENCE ON RUSSIAN HILL, 1985-89

NOTES ON POST-MODERNISM

I think it appropriate to start with some comments on the term Post-Modernism and my use of it.[1] I adopted the term as a result of some discussions with Peter Eisenman in 1975. Eisenman pointed out that while it was perfectly clear that he and I were both against the same things, we were not in favour of the same things. That is, we were both concerned with the break-up of the seemingly monolithic Modern Movement; and we were both contemptuous of the kind of stylish, appliqué Modernism that we saw around us as well as the anti-architectural philistinism that was the unfortunate by-product of the student movements of the late 1960s. I was only too familiar with the latter, as much from teaching experiences at Columbia as from my own student days at Yale where its earliest manifestations could be seen in the back-to-the-woods, architec-ture-as-act movements of the 60s. Though Eisenman and I ap-proached the situation from quite opposite points of view, we each saw the so-called revolutionary conditions of architecture of the 60s as ideologically confused, artistically debilitated, nihilistic and anti-intellectual. Although these student movements supplied a necessary critisism of the then current scene and made obvious the hypocrisy that afflicted our national political attitudes towards the war in Vietnam and the situation of minorities at home, they hadn't led to anything positive in terms of architectural production. What had begun as a useful critique of a situation proved unable to develop a positive direction of its own; it had no firm commitment to form-making or even a coherent political or social programme. It was against things but not for things.

Eisenman by 1975 had evolved a point of view which was positive in its insistence that the ideals of utilitarian functionalism and technological determinism had hopelessly compromised the formalist intentions of the initiating architects of the Modern Movement and had reduced that movement to a commercial exercise. He labelled his position 'post-functionalism', and sug-gested that my position, which was of course an outgrowth of the work of Charles Moore and Robert Venturi, was Post-Modern. By Post-Modern, I believe Eisenman really meant anti-Modern Move-ment; moreover I think he hoped it might also be against the Western humanist tradition. But as I see it, the term really describes a condition that comes after, and is in reaction to the Modern Movement and attempts to effect a synthesis between it and other strains of the Western humanist tradition.

In any case, I adopted the term as a useful label, only to find, just after I went 'public' with it at an *Oppositions* forum in January 1976, that Charles Jencks was bringing out a book, *The Language of Post-Modern Architecture*[2] which dealt with the same subject. This discovery, though initially annoying, was in the long run consoling: I was no longer the only person to believe that Modernism was finished and that a new synthesis, a devolution and *not* a revolu-tion, was well under way.

Though Jencks' book is quite wonderful in many ways, it fails to define very precisely, if at all, just what Post-Modernism is. It also does not make any connections between Post-Modernism in architecture and the use of the term to describe similar (but by no means identical) movements in the other visual arts as well as music and literature. Its weaknesses and its strengths helped to define my position and outline a course of action; as a result, I

undertook a cross-disciplinary investigation of Post-Modernist tendencies that resulted in the essay, 'The Doubles of Post-Modern'.[3]

Arnold Toynbee appears to have made the earliest significant use of the term in his *Study of History*[4] of 1954. Toynbee's argu-ment on behalf of a Post-Modern period was developed by Geoffrey Barraclough in his book, *An Introduction to the Idea of Contemporary History*.[5] For Barraclough, the Post-Modern period, whose origins he sets at about 1870-1890, marked a radical break with the modern, or Western humanist, tradition; and a new 'contemporary' history replaced the existing modern history which he believed had begun in the modern period (which, though imprecisely defined in architectural historiography, I accept as having begun around 1450).

I believe the Post-Modern/contemporary phenomenon described by Barraclough does not represent a break from the modern tradition but is rather a new phase within it. The modern period still exists and thrives. Culturally and politically we have not yet arrived at that state of true pluralism in which the Western humanist value system is only one among others of equal impor-tance in the world – a state which Barraclough claims as essential to the definition of the new Post-Modern period; and in architec-ture I would say that the same is true. So what we have is architecture still grounded in the modern tradition but with the existence of two phases: Modernism and Post-Modernism, each quite different from the other. Modernism was an attitude towards the making of things that sought to free itself from any reference to the past, but went further by its rejection of historical values and advocacy of change at all cost. For Modernism, the past merely served to define a negative condition: new is better. Having cut the thread of historical continuity insofar as artistic production is concerned, the Modernist had no sources for his art outside the circumstances of its commissioning and the wellspring of his own perceptions. As a result, Modernist art is at once materialistically determined and self-referential. Modernism's rejection of histori-cal retention set each new work of art adrift to make its own independent iconic claim. Post-Modernism, on the other hand, does not reject Modernism and its monuments in the that way Modernism rejected all previous stylistic movements – Romanti-cism particularly, but also the Renaissance, Baroque and Rococo – however Post-Modernism does reject the anti-historical stance of Modernism and its cult of newness. Post-Modernism in architec-ture argues that the modern period is characterised by competing ideas that co-exist: eclecticism, associationalism, representation, abstraction and non-representation.

Ours is a culture torn between the urge to jettison the past and start anew and an urge to link up in as many ways as possible with the past in order to ameliorate the impact of the radical changes which science and technology have thrust upon us. Post-Modern-ism accepts this contradictory condition whereas Modernism does not. Post-Modernism holds out the possibility of a truly inclusive philosophy of action that will accommodate the condition of the present to the values society believes were embodied in the past and which it wishes to carry forward. As a philosophical condition, Post-Modernism is difficult to describe because one always wants to define things by saying what they are not. But to define a philosophical condition by saying that it represents an acknowledgment of everything, that it is, in essence, permissive and not restrictive, opens one up to the jibes of those who confuse permissiveness with moral and intellectual laxity. For Peter Eisenman, for example, permissive is a nasty, pejorative term. Eisenman argues that he is the first true Modernist and in a certain way I think he's right. He has really thrown out everything from architecture except the object, and in his own work meaning comes from a confrontation between the viewer and the object.

– You wouldn't include early De Stijl architecture as a source for Eisenman's work, then?

The work of De Stijl architects and sculptors such as Vantongerloo is, of course, a source, but its implications for architecture as opposed to sculpture are not so extreme. It does not go nearly so far as Eisenman's – it isn't nearly as abstract. Next to Eisenman's House VI, Rietveld's Schroeder House looks like a sales model for National Homes: it's a real house! Or at least it comes close to being one, with a bottom and top, front and back, and all kinds of literal flexibility – and it doesn't have a slot severing the conjugal bed. It is positively accommodating; primitively functionalist from Eisenman's point of view, I suppose.

– Do you feel that Eisenman's is a valuable gesture to make at this time and place?

I think it's an interesting last gasp, an extreme cry on behalf of Modernism. But it poses a dilemma for Eisenman: what to do next? House X, which is not going to be built, seems to be just a further complication of the ideas explored in House VI. An important question, that Eisenman's work raises and one implicit in the reductionism that is part of Modernism, remains: what is the value of the object after all concern with utility and commodity and representation is omitted from the design process, when architecture is left naked and pure? Eisenman's last-gasp Modernism comes at a time when Modernism in the other arts is already under considerable attack.

In art criticism, for example, the term Post-Modernism has been used since the 1960s, principally to describe a direction of thinking that rejects the absoluteness of Clement Greenberg's claims about what he believes is the inherent non-representational nature of painting and sculpture. Brian O'Doherty, Gregory Battcock, Calvin Tompkins and Rackstraw Downes each use the term Post-Modernism in important ways. Though none of them has defined it precisely, Downes[6], in his essay 'Tracks', on behalf of realism brings the argument quite close to my own. Modernism's anti-representational stance has reduced painting and sculpture to gestural arts in which craft has disappeared; as a result it has become very difficult to distinguish the empty gestures from those that are redolent with meaning. The seeds of the Post-Modernist 'devolution' in art were sown in the late 1950s in the work of Robert Rauschenberg and Jasper Johns: not only is their use of recognisable imagery important, but their mixing of media represents a rejection of Modernism's search for the essence of any given art form – pure painting, for example, as Clement Greenberg defines it.

– Are you suggesting that it's even more difficult to achieve the Greenbergian goal of purity or essence in architecture because you rely on buildings to serve some function, some external purpose outside themselves? And that Eisenman's search for pure architecture is a step backwards? Might it also be true that if Eisenman was pursuing Greenberg's goal, he was going in the wrong direction? His buildings don't strike me as notable titillations for the architectural eye because they ignore so much of what architecture needs to do.

Greenberg's rigid and exclusivist insistence on Modernist painting as the essence of painting, as pure painting, represents an extreme point of view that is sustained in the work of only a very few artists, most of whom I think are decorative but dull: Olitski, Newman, Davis. Most Modernist painters cling to some form of representation – whether it is Mondrian's syncopated grids that depict the boogie-woogie or Jackson Pollock's calligraphic gestures that render visible the processes of art. Representation in painting and in the other arts is at once a source of pleasure (if only in what Edmund Wilson described in another context as 'the shock of recognition') and a way to communicate meaning. Modernist architecture tended to substitute Utopianism for representationalism; it focused its energies on the world as it might be and often lost sight of and interest in the world as it is.

While I would agree that architecture has to have a Utopian ambition, I do not think it need be as single-minded a vision as it was. A Post-Modernist Utopia would be one in which the various cultures would co-exist while each would retain its meaning and character. Frank Lloyd Wright, Le Corbusier and Ebenezer Howard, three major Utopian speculators of this century, were pretty explicit about how people should live, what they should do, where they should brush their teeth, everything. I think many views of Utopia are wall-to-wall impossible, tyrannical in the most basic sense. I don't mean to throw out idealism, but an idealism that is based not on an improvement of what exists but on a radical imposition of something new is a form of totalitarianism. Progress is not really so dead as the philosophy of progress has made it appear to be. I think that it is part of the human condition to have an ameliorative urge, a progressive urge. But I think the idea of progress as its own reward, which was a pretty hot idea in the late 19th century, is probably dead. We know that some kinds of progress bring almost as many problems as possibilities. Whilst Modernism failed to recognise the retrogressive implications of material progress, Post-Modernism attempts to measure progress relative to its absence.

Post-Modernism has been described as a naive throwback to 19th-century positivism. This is not so: the 19th century believed in progress as its own reward; the Post-Modernist sees progress as a relative process. The idea that small is beautiful is a Post-Modernist one. One of our contemporary dilemmas is that an intelligent person cannot act outside history. The concept of history is really a concept of the modern period. It is the background against which we operate; modernity is the condition by which action in the present is measured in relationship to similar actions in the past. Modernism tries to escape from history but not from modernity. Despite their rejection of history, the advocates of Modernism knew that history was closing in on them. They felt its terrible weight and they couldn't get away from it. I don't believe you can ever escape history; as Philip Johnson ruefully pointed out to architects at Yale in the 1950s, you cannot not know history.

Post-Modernism is a frame of mind. It's a phase of history, a mood. And it's definitely here. Maybe it would be better if we called it 'blue' or something. But it is a phase and though someday it may have a proper name of its own, we're stuck with this 'Post-Modern' one at least for now.

Post-Modernism embodies a kind of relativist inclusive position, a permissiveness in the sense that everything can find its own level and its own expression, that each thing has its own value, and that the architect's job or society's job is to weigh and balance these things to make relationships. The very fact that today we can talk about buildings having meanings apart from those specifically related to functional accommodation and technological resolution – without anyone screaming in agony – confirms that our architectural culture has shifted from the Modernist to the Post-Modernist: Modernist architects would never acknowledge that buildings had built-in meanings. Gropius said that buildings were basically constructs to solve functional problems in relationship to technology, that they took on a style as a result of observations made from without. We recognise that when we make something, we consciously manipulate existing meanings, and that in the act of making we understand that the meanings might or might not change, that our work might add or subtract from them or modify those meanings. We think about meaning; we do not wait for society to assign meanings to our work, although on the other hand, we recognise that it will do so in time and that those meanings will become part of the meaning of the building we have designed.

– One thing that bothers me is the dilemma that seems to arise from our need to make distinctions and our inability to really believe in those distinctions.

I think your dilemma is part of our inheritance from Modernism; we're all trained in Modernism, though this is much less true for students today than for their teachers. For example, the way we study art history is affected by Modernist dialectic: two slides; this one or that, one slide usually represents one set of values and the other represents its opposite. We are programmed to see art as a dialectic when it isn't that simple, is it? The urge to make categories is a modern obsession; the codification of knowledge in terms of values – good guys and bad guys – is Modernist.

A movement is not really a style. The Modern Movement (which I consider to be the polemicising arm of Modernism) was about a lot of ideas which found their most complete expression in the International Style, the Classicising formal language which emerged in the 1920s. There were other styles that were equally involved in the ideas of the Modern Movement, but were not as expressive or as potent; more importantly, they were considered anti-Classical, and the Classical taste is the dominant one in Western humanism. The origins of Post-Modernism in architecture can be traced to the 1950s. Important milestones include the publication of Henry Russell Hitchcock's *Architecture, Nineteenth and Twentieth Century*,[7] which revealed the complexity of the period under discussion and shattered many myths fostered by Giedion and Pevsner; Reyner Banham's *Theory and Design in the First Machine Age*,[8] which drew open the curtain that the polemicists of the CIAM had dropped over certain Modernist experiments in the 1920s that did not conform to their conception of what the new architecture should be; Vincent Scully's *Shingle Style*[9] which represented a stylistic movement in the modern period that was as clearly articulated and as pervasive, as inventive and as responsive to tradition as the Rococo or the Baroque, but which integrated Classicism and vernacularism in a way that had only the example of Palladio as a precedent.

Post-Modernist design was anticipated by Eero Saarinen, who sensed the limitations of the minimalism and non-representationalism of the International Style. Saarinen was misunderstood by his contemporaries such as Minoru Yamasaki and Edward D Stone, who parodied his intentions. Yet his TWA terminal at Kennedy Airport, the Dulles Airport outside Washington DC, Bell Labs, and Stiles and Morse Colleges at Yale are each an embodiment of Saarinen's belief in the 'style for the job', and as such are important precursors of Post-Modernism. Intimations of Post-Modernist design can also be seen in the writings and some projects of Matthew Nowicki, who worked with Saarinen on the early proposals for Brandeis University, Nowicki was a Pole who was stranded here as a result of the Second World War. He was to have designed Chandigarrh but was killed in an aeroplane crash in Egypt on a trip to the site. Like Saarinen, Nowicki had begun to question the presumptions of the Modern Movement. I think most of us do not now find Nowicki's architecture and sketches to our taste. The buildings are late 1940s, structural handstands in their approach. Even the writings are probably more important in the context of their historical position than on their own terms.

So much for the precursors of Post-Modernism and its broad premises. What are its beliefs? How are they expressed in bricks and mortar? The article 'Drawing Toward a More Modern Architecture' in *Architectural Design*[10] was my first attempt at establishing a definition for Post-Modernism that would be neither prescriptive, nor proscriptive (as Hitchcock and Johnson's had been for the International Style[11]), nor so vague and amorphous as to render the term meaningless or permissive in the pejorative sense. Contextualism, allusionism and ornamentalism are each strategies for re-introducing into architecture qualities that Modernism had deliberately thrown out. In my *Architectural Design* article I listed three hallmarks of the Post-Modernist sensibility: contextualism, allusiveness and ornamentalism. These hallmarks are culturally and perceptually oriented, unlike those of Modernism (functionalism, technological determinism, Utopianism), which are pragmatic and ideological.

– How can you argue that there's any more validity in the cultural function of architecture than in its pragmatic function?

Virtually all buildings in the history of architecture have been pretty much based in pragmatism – that is, in problem-solving. Whether it is a pharaoh in need of a tomb or a 19th-century robber-baron in need of a palace, a building begins with a programme. But utilitarian programmes repeat themselves. More importantly, despite the emergence of so many new programmes and problems, most building types of our time have been largely carried forward from antiquity with only a very few innovations: the dome set on top of the basilica at Florence, the solid mass interrupting the basilica in the Prairie House of Frank Lloyd Wright, the skyscraper, the giant shed uninterrupted by internal supports at the Galerie des Machines. In any case, I don't think you can base a style on issues of function. Though style is not based on utilitarian pragmatism, it is a utilitarian device; style has function. It is the culturally responsive part of design.

– This is in regard to another issue. In talking about the British Art Center at Yale, you have said that one of the ways you might go about judging whether you thought it was a good or appropriate building was how closely it conformed to what was expected of a given type of building for its utilitarian and cultural purpose. What exactly do you mean by that?

The BAC is a very interesting case in point at this time. When I was in architecture school, Louis Kahn's work exemplified a number of ideals, principally the one concerning integration of structural and spatial concerns to make spaces of great integrity. Kahn also reintroduced historical architecture as a direct source of inspiration in the design process. But Kahn's use of history was abstract and personal; his buildings never looked like their models. For Kahn, history was meaningful on a personal as opposed to a cultural level. The history of the cultures which permitted him to build bore no particular role in his process of design. You remember that when Kahn learned that brick was the most suitable material for building in India and Pakistan, he asked brick what it wanted to be and it revealed to him that it wanted to be an arch. What is interesting is that after this conversation Kahn did look at brick architecture, articulated or otherwise, but not the brick architecture of the Indian subcontinent. Kahn turned to examples from Ostia Antica, a place which is part of the Western European tradition that he related to, but which is quite exotic for the ultimate users of the buildings he was about to design.

The self-referential aspect of Kahn's work characterises the design of the BAC as well. On the exterior the building makes no effort to represent any aspect of its purpose; only the process of its making. And in the interior, the character of the display rooms is quite remote from the kinds of rooms that existed when the art in the permanent collection was originally made. Our expectations for a building that would establish an appropriate context for the work of Stubbs and his contemporaries is only barely acknowledged by the use of wood panelling, which is treated as though it were a finer form of plasterboard and not as though it were a part of the tradition of Grinling Gibbons. Stubbs wants to be hung cheek by jowl with others, not isolated inside a 'white' cube like Mondrian.

I am arguing for an architecture that is at once timeless and timely. Kahn's building is universal in its intentions; I am arguing for one that is specific and universal, one that deals in the eternal verities of light, structure and space which Kahn understood so well, and that *also* deals in the responsive or communicative aspects of style – not personal style but cultural style. The BAC is as it is because Kahn's ideas about architecture were as they were, not because the purposes of the building – the sympathetic presentation of a significant collection of historical art – was as it was. The BAC is a marvellous building, a key work of Modernist art. In its way, it is perfect and wonderful, but is its way our way? In its search for rules broad enough to fit all exceptions, as Sullivan put it, is it subtle enough to mark the distinctions and differences that make each situation, each work of art it contains, a unique moment to be savoured for its own sake?

– The wooden panelling was supposed to be referential to a certain time and place. Do you think that it was just not sufficiently characterised?

I've never been in an English country house in which Alvar Aalto had done the panelling.

– Do you think the art really suffers?

Yes, the best place to see the art in the BAC is in the store-rooms up at the top where the paintings are hung on racks one next to the other and one atop the other. Images are jumbled-up and the result looks quite like a picture gallery in a country house of the 18th and early 19th centuries as they are depicted in paintings from the period. You can't put a dinky little picture of a dog on a vast wall and expect it to have the iconographic importance of a Raphael or a Mondrian. As an artist, Stubbs accepted the fact that his paintings would be hung as part of a 'mosaic' of painted images; that his was an intimate, incidental art, not a transcendent one.

– But do you think you could extend that argument and say that one of the ways of judging buildings in general is to see how much they conform to what is expected of them?

Yes.

– Do you think that such a standard would be a kind of strange version of functionalism?

Cultural functionalism not utilitarian functionalism.

– Could it be that Kahn was not trying to make the universal kind of Modernist space. Maybe he was trying to make an atemporal thing? In other words, might it be possible to disassociate the building from how it is outfitted for a particular performance?

But why do that? In Kahn's gallery in Fort Worth, the Kimball Art Museum, which is a marvellous building housing an eclectic collection of art from all periods, the universal space created is functional from both the utilitarian and cultural point of view. The BAC, with its relatively fixed collection, suffers from Kahn's unwillingness to shift from the general to the particular; or rather, to include both the general and the particular. Probably this issue didn't occur to Kahn. Though he professed interest in the circumstantial, the ideal of the particular was outside Kahn's view of architecture. Take another case from the Yale campus – the display of American chairs from the 18th, 19th and 20th centuries in the Garvan Collection of the Yale Art Gallery. In this display (which I think was designed by Ivan Chermayeff), all the chairs are exhibited as though contemporary with one another. The exhibit seems to say that a chair is a chair is a chair . . . and while this is true in the generic sense it trivialises the role of the chair in a cultural sense. The same could be said of the human bottoms which the chairs support; it is true that an ass is an ass is an ass . . . but the differences of heft and carriage across time not to mention from person to person are what is really interesting. *Vive la différence!*

– But it seems to me that if you go beyond that and extend the argument to other things, then at some point you have to start dealing with the question of what value is the unexpected and what could be reasonable grounds for using it.

The way you say the word 'unexpected' brings us back to the Modernist idea that a work of art is good if it is shocking; that somehow it is better if the viewer doesn't know what a work of art is about, if the viewer has to learn to understand it and therefore to admire it.

– You're guilty of it.

Oh, I may be – yes, that's perfectly true.

– I'll bet you don't like surprises.

Well, there are all kinds of surprises. There's the kind of surprise you get when you go to a movie expecting to see a musical with fabulous dancing and it turns out to have been even more fabulous than you had ever imagined. And then there's another kind of surprise you get when the marquee proclaims a musical but the film turns out to be an Ingmar Bergman musical, not very musical!

– There's a distinction between shock and surprise.

We have now had 100 years of the self-perpetuating avant-garde. Harold Rosenberg called it the 'tradition of the new'.[12] The idea of perpetual shock has become an institutionalised phenomenon in art, not without some jeopardy to the production of meaning. If an artist always feels he has to do something new, then what's the point of studying history, or of being educated at all except insofar as to master a craft, and even that is not very important when the shock value of novelty is held in higher esteem than the refinement of the object itself. Donald Judd has designed sculptures which he has had constructed over the telephone. What's the point of ever looking around? Why not go home and stare at your navel and wait for art to erupt from your inner self? This cult of the new, in which the new is defined as the difficult, is exactly what some of us have been struggling to overcome in the last 20 years. I think the hardest part of it is to admit that when confronted with the task of producing a building for a collection of 18th- and 19th-century horse and dog pictures, you might make rooms very close to the kinds of rooms architects of the late 18th century made, as close as you can get in fact . . .

– I think you could make an argument, though, that you have to design from what you know. And if you don't know anything, then I wonder what happens? You're just in a sort of vacuum as opposed to being in a situation where you have all this historical information to draw on.

I don't think it's enough to design from what you know unless you know everything. As an architect you must become a scholar; you must make the effort to find out what is expected of a building as well as what is the point of origin of a given set of circumstances that cause a building to be commissioned. You have to find out what's expected of you by the client, by society, by history. As an architect you must not rest on a concern for the plumbing or the latest technological innovation or whatever. You should find out what the culture expects of a particular building.

– I think what's bothering people is that doing precisely what is expected of you sounds entirely too much like feeding your mother.

What's wrong with feeding your mother? Can't you please your mother and grow up? Why on earth has it come to be accepted that if you please your mother you don't grow up, but if you don't please your mother you do grow up? I think that's ridiculous. I think the problem is that you are preoccupied with originality. Why don't you get it right out on the table, you are nervous because you believe that in order to make it, you need to come forward with an unexpected, unprecedented, unfamiliar, idiosyncratic formal statement.

– What you are saying has a lot to do with the word that you were using. To me at least, you can change the word 'unexpected' into such words as 'new', 'startling', 'bold'. To me, unexpected needn't mean new.

I agree. So say a new thing, by combining the words of the language in a new way; to make a subtle modification of what had been thought to be a closed issue, is to do the unexpected. To shout an obscenity or to ignore all known rules of grammar and syntax is to shock.

– To shift to another building type, another aspect of the problem, I was wondering about what one should do, what you do, when people expect a kind of building, say a bank, that is to be built in a charming historical district to be new and sleek and modern?

The Modernist styles, and especially the International Style, have already acquired meanings. The International Style, now has a firmly established set of meanings and it can be used as deliberately and as self-consciously as the Gothic or the Doric or whatever. The bank is a particularly interesting case in point. From the time of Soane through that of McKim, the urban bank was almost exclusively associated with the traditional, Classical language of architecture, and especially with a strict representation of the orders on the principal facade. Since the time of Gordon Bunshaft's Manufacturers Hanover Bank in New York, the language of banks has been Modernist Classical, and especially associated with Miesian vocabulary. This is particularly interesting given the anticapitalist intentions of many of the progenitors of Modernism in architecture; but since the time of Bunshaft, that is since the emergence of the second and largely American generation of Modernist architects, the original associations of the language have been cast out in favour of a new and opposite set of values. I shall not go into the trivialisation of Miesian form which accompanied this process and which led one wag in the late 1950s to label Bunshaft's firm of Skidmore Owings and Merrill as 'Three Blind Mies'.

The case of Edwin Lutyens' Westminster Bank on Piccadilly in London offers some interesting comments on the issue of a new building in an historical context. Lutyens' bank is located on a site adjoining Sir Christopher Wren's St James Church. In deference to Wren's work, Lutyens designed the bank in the style of the church; it flanks the churchyard in a harmonious way, yet it is a fresh design which is remarkably interesting in its own right. Now, if one of us were to get the commission for the Westminster Bank today – say it had been destroyed by bombs during the Second World War – how would we handle it? I would say that one would have to find a way to design a bank that satisfied the bank's image of itself as efficient, approachable, 'up-to-date' while at the same time satisfying the culture's demands that Wren's building be honoured. I would even suggest that the memory of Lutyens building be honoured too, not only because its (hypothesised) destruction is a monument to the folly of war but also because the building represented something fine in its own right. To do this, one would have to be eclectic in the best sense. One would have to be able to speak of Wren and Lutyens and Mies; one would have to be something of an architectural linguist – that is, a scholar, which used to be the model of the architect before the Romantic era with its emphasis on personal invention.

So to those who worry about making things that look 'modern', that is contemporary, new, particular to our time, or whatever, I say relax. Take care of architecture and let the *Zeitgeist* take care of itself. While it is folly to imagine that the past can be brought into the present, one can quite productively imagine what the past might have been like and include those imaginings in the formulations of the present. A building of our time is automatically a representation of our time.

– Do you think that this kind of elaborate sensitivity to context is a fairly recent phenomenon or one which existed prior to Modernism?

I think good architects have always responded to the context of their work. Even in Modernism, despite its iconoclasm, the references, as in Le Corbusier's use of pipe rails and other machine products, to cite a typical example, were from outside architecture.

– It seems you are saying that the culture of the present time is tending to foster the establishment of a compound style. Do you think this tendency toward hybridisation is an aspect of only our time, or is it characteristic of the bigger modern continuum?

The Modern period is characterised by the production of art in relationship to the past; it is characterised by an eclectic process which is not known to have existed before the Renaissance. Modernism eliminated historicism, but it did not eliminate eclecticism; it chose its icons from outside architecture. The Shingle-Style and free-style architects of the late 19th century were not interested in literal use of historical language, but they were in favour of historical influence. These styles drew upon earlier architecture just as virtually every important architectural style has since the Classical language was revived in the 15th century on the basis of an eclectic integration of elements from the past. As a design strategy, eclecticism becomes increasingly difficult and interesting the further along we come in history. There is so much more to learn from and so many more meanings that it is more difficult to determine what to choose or at least what to relate to. Because we have access to so much past, we may become surfeited by it. This happened in the 1920s, and the purgative that was the Modern Movement, though possibly necessary, was a bit harsh. Its perpetuation for 50 or more years was surely disruptive to the natural processes of digestion.

– Well, just let me add this, that the reaction to the contextual brutality of modern architecture has tended to bring into the picture incredibly soft attitudes toward things like preservation, for example: 'That building is 70 years old or 90 years old, and it's just got to be there – and God help what we do if we ever start to tear it down.' Well, that is a kind of peculiar attitude, though perhaps it can be seen as a kind of over-reaction to the excess of Modernism. I'm wondering if forms of contextualism are also an over-reaction, a kind of guilt over the lack of contextual sense in modern architecture?

I think the preservation movement is very much a Post-Modernist phenomenon. Preservation would have been unimaginable 25 years ago. One reason preservation has become so popular is because people so distrust what might be built as replacement for an old building, or in fact have various grave and perfectly logical doubts that anything ever will be built at all. New Haven is a fine testament to the wisdom of these popularly held suspicions. The Hill neighbourhood might have become horribly run-down, but it was certainly better than the empty land which replaces it at the edges of downtown New Haven. The public is concerned that even an ordinary building from the past (or at least one built of nice materials) will be replaced by something that will be both ordinary and junky (built of absolute ersatz), or perhaps even worse, it might be replaced by one so offensively extraordinary that it looks like a building doing a handstand. Another thing about preservation is that, from an architect's point of view, and from the point of view of style, it brings us back in another way to the issues raised by Lou Kahn's building. We save these old buildings and then we proceed to remodel them in a way that is brutalising to their inherent qualities. For example, the newly resuscitated Quincy Market in Boston causes one to ask, 'For this they saved it? To sell wax candles?' And the renovation of the interior of Richardson's railroad station in New London, Connecticut, is absolutely illiterate. The Art and Architecture building at Yale, with its millions of faults, did not deserve the brutal renovations it has received. It is a work of art which has been outrageously trashed.

Part of the problem of 'preservation architecture' lies with architects who have been brought up in the tradition of '*Zeitgeist* determinism'. These architects feel they must do something different because the times are different. So though they may argue that Richardson's station is great and that Richardson was a great architect, they are unwilling to subsume their own talents to the master's. We should measure the accomplishment of a work of historic preservation by a yardstick that takes into consideration our best and most scholarly estimate of what the original architect would have done, given the new programme) but not necessarily given the new moment of history). It's easy to joke about the new International Preservationist style of exposed brick walls, butcher block, ferns and candles, but who will save our buildings from these preservers?

– You seem to suggest that contextual responsiveness requires stylistic reproduction, or at least hybridisation. Yet many of our most coherent urbanistic groupings incorporate buildings in many different styles.

Architecture can be contextually responsive in many ways. In addition to stylistic coherence, there is compositional congruence. If you're Hugh Hardy and you are building a bit of infill in a Greek Revival row in New York, is it appropriate to introduce a skewered bay window on the facade, even if you have otherwise quite faithfully reproduced the formal language of the row? If you're HH Richardson and you're building in the Harvard Yard, can you make a new building that is at once a direct re-statement of the original Georgian dormitory buildings in the Yard and a new statement that responds to a different functional programme as well as to your own personal style? In this light it is interesting to compare Richardson's Sever Hall in the Yard with his Austen Hall for Harvard Law School, which is located on what was in the 1880s a newly opened portion of the campus outside the Yard. Sever Hall is a work of contextual responsiveness; Austen is a far more abstract statement, Sever is for me the greater work. It is personal and contextual; it is a revival and a survival and in these ways a true innovation. I think it is true that in certain great cities buildings relate to each other by a sense of proportion and materials; relationships which are more abstract than representational. But if one part of the Rue de Rivoli were blown up, would you come in and rebuild it in a new way or would you rebuild the facade in the traditional style? The latter would be the only thing I could do. It's absurd to think otherwise.

– The Rue de Rivoli is a special case. That's a kind of a set piece.

Well, the Greek Revival streetscape on 11th Street where Hugh Hardy is building is special also; it is virtually the only one of its kind remaining in Manhattan.

If you build on a typical suburban street where all the houses have front lawns and little walks and garages and pitched roofs and shutters, and maybe one house is in Georgian and so on, to me you don't come along and build a Villa Savoye – not so much because it does not fit in stylistically but because it does not fit compositionally. On the other hand, how do you add on to the Villa Savoye? What can one do? I think the courteous thing to do would be to make something sympathetic, even deferential. That's a good studio problem, right? It goes with my other wonderful fantasy which asks that one add on to the Villa Savoye because the family has gotten a divorce and there are now more kids and Mrs Savoye (who kept the house) is remarried. The point is that instead of the monolithic attitude of the Modern Movement's International Style, which argued that we have a way of building, that the *Zeitgeist* has us all sewn up, can't we say that there are many ways?

– The overt reference to a particular style sometimes seems to recall not so much that style as other overt references. For example, period rooms in some museums remind one more of model rooms in department stores where they're trying to sell period furniture, than interiors of the period intended to be illustrated.

Some department stores do things very well.

– I'm not questioning that they do. I think that they do it well and that fast food and popular culture people also do their thing well.

What I think you're getting at is what I'd describe as the 'how are you gonna keep 'em back in Oxford and Cambridge after they've seen Yale's Branford College' syndrome. You never can do it 'straight' any more. You can't go back. It's impossible. You can never go to Cambridge or Oxford and see them fresh once you have been to Branford College. It's so much better at Branford: cleaned up, perfect, spatially regularised, it's marvellous. You can never look at the original straight, and that's one of our modern problems. But how, also, can you look at the International Style any more after you've taken a drive down Route 66? After you've seen it used for gas stations and Caldor's? The point is, we must draw back and think about what it all means again. This is a true crisis, a perpetual on-going crisis in our society. Williamsburg looks like the Harvard residential houses of the 30s because the same architects who were restoring Williamsburg were building the Harvard houses.

As an architect I am not offended by commercialism; I am only offended by the disjunction between the moralising Modernist ethos and its rather cynical accommodation to commercial realities. By this I refer to the situation which occurred in the 1950s when Gropius and other pioneer Modernists began to build large-scale commercial buildings and to assign holy values to their work. Gropius' defence of his role in the design of the Pan American building in New York, in which he claimed that by virtue of his intervention, New York was spared a vulgar product of crass commercialism, was self-serving to say the least. Scully has shown us in an article in *Perspecta*[13] that Gropius' interference actually made the project worse! And Marcel Breuer's arguments in defence of his proposals for a tower atop Grand Central Terminal in New York are, if possible, even more appalling.

– Do you eat at McDonald's?

Yes, sometimes. The great thing about a pluralistic world is that you can eat lunch at McDonald's and go to La Grenouille at night and not feel hypocritical. Craig Claiborne can write an article about the qualities of fast food one day in *The Times*, and the next day he can write about something as esoteric as truffles, and you don't think he's sold out. But can you imagine Walter Gropius talking positively about the pleasures of McDonald's architecture? I can't. And so I'm encouraged. We don't have a way of doing things. That's the wonderful thing about our time. And like it or not, you can't escape its pluralism. And I personally don't see why you would want to. There are many ways – there is always room for any position. But I think you would be naive to believe that there ever really was a single way: Gropius' great frustration was that it never all came to pass. White Dusenbergs, or Adlers to be more precise, didn't take over the world. I don't know what he thought about himself when it was all finished, but there is quite a shift of intentions from the high ideals of the Bauhaus to the work of the Architects' Collaborative. He must have thought a little bit about this shift. It's pretty sad, it seems to me.

– You said that right now there's no one way to do anything. What interests me was you said 'right now'; do you think you're going to live out your life with what you're saying now being valid?

Let me put it this way. I don't believe there has ever been one way of doing architecture in what I define in the broadest terms as the Modern period, and certainly not since the 18th century. So there is not any particular reason to believe there is going to be one way until, without getting too ridiculous, there is some radical change in the nature of our culture and our world.

– Well, do you think, for instance that the literature on Post-Modernism will be useful except as historical documents 10 years from now, 20 years from now, 30 years from now?

I like to think so, yes. I like to believe that, given how long it has taken architectural ideas to unfold and take root in the past, this Post-Modern phase is to be with us for the rest of this century. It takes a while. The Modern Movement had its origins in the 1830s and reached a peak in the 1920s; and it is still going to be creaking along for quite a while. Paul Rudolph is about to begin to build the new New Haven City Hall, hardly a Post-Modern building. It's probably going to be a very nice building in its way, yet a lot of people are going to be very irritated about it because it will not embody certain attitudes that one believes in today. On the other hand, it is a building that was conceived ten or more years ago and which looked pretty good to the people who were thinking about buildings then. So all these ideas we're talking about – Modernist and Post-Modernist alike – are going to haunt us for better or for worse for quite a while to come.

At the moment, I am interested in the problem of literalness in architecture. The joking use of Doric columns, and other pieces of the Classical language as in Venturi's Art Museum at Oberlin College or in Charles Moore's Piazza d'Italia in New Orleans is one thing, but what about the straightforward use of this language? The traditional Classical language exists as do such newer ones as the International Style and the Art Deco. They are all interrelated and the distance of time between us and the battles of the 1920s may well give us enough breathing room to permit a synthesis to take place between them, comparable to the birth of English out of the Anglo and Romance languages of the Middle Ages.

Because I went to Yale in the 60s it has taken me a long time to figure out what I was taught I shouldn't do. We are all trapped by our education. I'm attempting to 'brainwash' my students as I was brainwashed by my teachers. I can talk faster than I can design. But it's awfully hard to teach clients. It is interesting that when they come to architects like me, they expect me to produce buildings that Arthur Drexler won't show any more at the Museum of Modern Art. You see, Modernism has become a fashion, a style with *cachet*. Many clients want their buildings to look like what modern architects are supposed to produce.

– So really there's a gap between what you think, what you design now and what people expect you to design.

I am always struggling to close those gaps.

Notes

1 This essay was prepared from tape-recordings of Robert AM Stern's visits to the *Issues in Architecture* seminar course at the Yale School of Architecture during January and Febuary of 1978, and first published in *Yale Seminars in Architecture* 1, ed by Cesar Pelli, Yale Univ Press, New Haven, 1981, pp 1-35.

2 Charles Jencks, *The Language of Post-Modern Architecture*, Academy Editions, London, first edition 1977, sixth edition 1991.

3 Robert AM Stern, 'The Doubles of Post-Modern', *Harvard Architectural Review*, 1, Spring 1980: 74-87.

4 Arnold Toynbee, *The Study of History*, Oxford University Press, 1954.

5 Geoffrey Barraclough, *Introduction to the Idea of Contemporary History*, Basic Books, New York, 1965.

6 Rackstraw Downes, 'Post-Modernist Painting', in *Tracks*, Vol II No 3, 1976.

7 Henry Russell Hitchcock, *Architecture, Nineteenth and Twentieth Century Architecture*, Penguin, Harmondsworth, 1971.

8 Reyner Banham, *Theory and Design in the First Machine Age*, Praeger, New York, 1960.

9 Vincent Scully, *Shingle Style*, Yale University Press, New Haven, 1955.

10 Robert AM Stern, 'Drawing Towards a More Modern Architecture', *Architectural Design*, Vol 47 No 6, 1977.

11 Henry Russell Hitchcock and Philip Johnson, *The International Style*, Norton, New York, 1966.

12 Harold Rosenberg, *The Tradition of the New*, Horizon Press, New York, 1959.

13 Vincent Scully, 'The Death of the Street', *Perspecta 8: The Yale Architectural Journal*, New Haven.

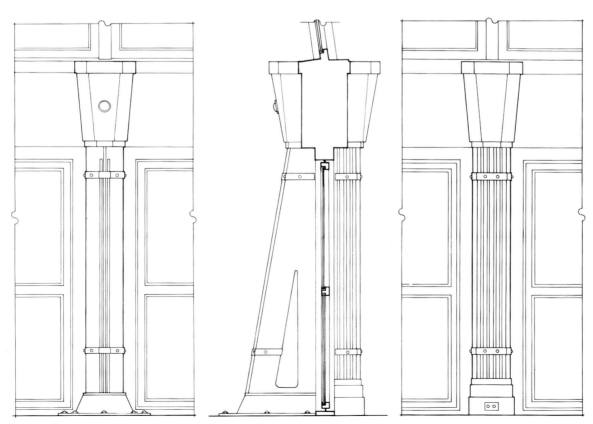

P 112: RESIDENCE AT MARBLEHEAD, 1984-87; *ABOVE*: MEXX INTERNATIONAL HEADQUARTERS, NETHERLANDS, 1985-87

ON STYLE, CLASSICISM AND PEDAGOGY

An architect cannot escape style.[1] I have never seen a building divorced from style, no matter how banal or inarticulate its expression. Every work of architecture represents an attempt to transcend mere shelter and accommodation. Building is specific, the literal translation of a programme into bricks and mortar. Architecture is general, raising building to a poetic level by embracing the cultural continuum: form and style, syntax and expression – they are the 'otherness' that lends building the resonance of art.

Every architect worthy of the name resorts to some chosen set of aesthetic rules. For these rules to operate in a culture they must respond to circumstances beyond the issues of budget, materials, function and – as importantly – the architect's own personality, and speak through a generally understood language. Form is the language of architecture. Style is interpretation.

Before the Modernist period, architectural style was the product of a *rapprochement* between building technology and Classicism. Matters have been complicated by the at least partial replacement of the craft tradition with industrialised production. Technology, hitherto the means of localising the general principles of Classicism through craft, became universal and a new, more self-conscious balance has had to be struck between principles and circumstance. Style can now be said to represent the interaction between elemental forms (Classicism) on the one hand and technology and the vernacular – the vernacular representing the sense of a specific place. This interactive process is at the heart of architectural narrative – for me the essence of architecture.

Architecture is a narrative art, and architectural style is analogous to poetic diction. Simple writing may literally communicate, but ordinarily does not give much pleasure. Story-tellers since the Greek tragedians have therefore embroidered their tales with references to, and even direct quotations from, works of the past to connect with tradition, not for its own sake but to deepen the experience of their art. The complexity of a narrative, its allusiveness, resonance and aggrandisement of the reader's own experience raise the statement of a simple literary theme to the realm of art.

One of the basic tenets of the 'Post-Modernist' reaction to Modernism is the reaffirmation of this narrative aspect: even so seemingly non-objective an architect as Peter Eisenman is preoccupied with story-telling. It is interesting to note that with Eisenman now building for more than one person, his narrative is moving from interior monologues to historical commentary, as in the castellated mock ruins of his project at Ohio State University. Contextual commentary has always been central to the communication of an architectural message, and I see no reason to abandon it now.

Enduring art cannot be founded on a negative statement. Art requires an assertion of belief. The initial impulse of paradigmatic Modernism was as much an iconoclastic attempt to destroy the concept of associative meaning in architecture as it was a positive glorification of the machine. But in actual practice, a crisis of style arose almost immediately. For Le Corbusier the traditional styles did not speak to the tumultuous issues of the day and were ingrained in a bourgeois culture which he abhorred. Yet in banishing historical representation he left himself little with which

to evolve a new style. At first he replaced the character of handicraft with that of machine production. Retaining the grid system of Classical composition he subverted it with diagonal and curved plan forms that were intended to represent the randomness of everyday life; the free plan was the antithesis of the Beaux-Arts *marche* with its connotations of hierarchy and stratification. Le Corbusier's initial vocabulary for the 'new architecture' – the ramp, the strip window, the pipe rail, etc – was simply a set of elements which were preferred because they flaunted Classical convention. By the 1930s, even Le Corbusier was frustrated by the restrictive 'purism' of his vocabulary and conscious of the futility of an art that refused to represent its past. His work thereafter sought to reconnect his art with the past. While it never satisfactorily came to terms with the monumental buildings of the Classical tradition, it does explore the vernacular of the Mediterranean.

The typical architect today builds all over the country and must vary the character of his buildings to suit the place. Frank Lloyd Wright varied his style, and, in doing so was not above making direct references to local historical styles. His buildings in Los Angeles are explicitly Mayan, a reflection of his desire to evolve an architecture appropriate to southern California while avoiding what he would have called the trap of Spanish Colonial. Yet he recognised in his writings the aptness of Spanish Colonial for that climate, with its courtyards, arcades and simple openings in unmodelled walls that capture the play of sunlight. His own work in the area was as historically referential as Goodhue's – where Goodhue turned to the evolved Classicism of the Spanish Colonial era, Wright went further back, to a near-mythic time before Columbus.

Wright's career represents an attempt to subsume Classicism into an intensely personal vision. The Imperial Hotel in Tokyo was his most extended dialogue between Classical composition and vernacular detail. Its rigorously symmetrical, hierarchical and sequentially organised plan, complete with traditional *cour d'honneur*, was a masterful essay in academic formalism. Designed for Westerners visiting Japan, the hotel drew upon Tuscany for inspiration: its low massing, tiled hipped roofs, and careful placement of representational ornament on a vernacular field reflect the influence of Wright's recent stay in Fiesole far more than any drive toward technological expressionism or study of local building traditions. The entrance pavilion in particular – in its proportions, its framed setting within a courtyard, and its straightforward use of rhetorical elements to transform a mundane box – preserved a distant, far-off echo of Brunelleschi's Pazzi Chapel.

The Larkin Building was a similarly distilled meditation on an Italian palazzo which intensified the typology's introverted focus on a glazed-in *cortile*. The ornament was rendered in Wright's own geometrical style, but its placement at the capitals and bases of piers was thoroughly Classical. All of Wright's successful public buildings save the Guggenheim Museum reflected the same command of Classical composition even if they rejected Classical details. After he lost the commission for the McCormick House to Charles Platt, Wright's major domestic designs sought the same synthesis. His project had called for a series of episodic, disconnected pavilions which failed to organise the extensive programme. Despite Wright's bitterness over the loss, I suspect he realised Platt had succeeded where he had failed. Thereafter his large houses were Classically composed suites of biaxially symmetrical rooms whose most significant innovation was the ubiquitous placement of hearth masses in the centre – a vernacular integration.

Wright's individualism was disciplined by his knowledge of tradition, demonstrated both by his Milwaukee Public Library project and his study of Lutyens. While one cannot study to become a highly personal talent like Wright (a common mistake of students in my generation), such a talent might emerge if one works from a tradition. Wright understood this perfectly. At Taliesin he set up a school in which students studied a tradition – not one culturally evolved from Classicism, but the personally willed tradition of his own work which he hoped to impose on the American people.

Classicism, as I see it, *is* the formal expression of modern (ie, Post-Medieval) secular institutions in the West. Classicism inherently represents the public and institutional realm, and the vernacular may be said to represent that which is private and temporal. Classicism has traditionally been used to transcend or modify the vernacular in order to draw people together in their diversity; it brings the Republican spirit of Washington to the county courthouses of the South and Midwest, just as it in turn brought the authority of Rome to cities meant to symbolise a nation – St Petersburg, New Delhi, Paris and Washington. The public realm, however, extends beyond great squares, museums and seats of government to encompass all levels of shared space. Classicism is not inherently identified with or tainted by any particular ideology, but has served rather as a distillation of the best that society can achieve. It is a tradition and a point of view. If, as some have suggested, even Monticello's Classicism is marred by the memory of slaves, what of Henry Bacon's Lincoln Memorial, whose testament to emancipation draws strength from a particular but nonetheless compelling interpretation of Greek democracy, and is further sanctified by memories of Martin Luther King and Marian Anderson, each of whom chose it as a forum? Great works of architecture, as surely as those of literature, painting and music, transcend the particular social or political situation in which they were created. To say otherwise requires that we dismiss all art of the past, and indeed the present moment, and idly wait for social conditions to improve.

Classicism is the only codified, amplified and perennially vital system of architectural composition bringing order to the process of design. It is also the only codified, amplified and perennially vital language of architectural form. Gothic is equally representational and widely admired, but it was a short-lived system, inextricably connected to a narrower set of associations and without a fully developed compositional system of its own. Modernism – that is, Functionalism – set out to do away with both associative meaning and the very concept of architectural grammar. It therefore possesses only the most minimal of resources to establish or vary character, and its compositional technique was based on behaviourism and a literal-minded interpretation of construction. Classicism is at once a tradition and a language incorporating rules of syntax and rhetoric; it provides a methodology to establish composition and character.

Classicism, as Lutyens argued, is 'the high game' of architecture. It presents the designer with a system of symphonic complexity for relating the smallest detail to the overall structure. It is the most abstract and complex language an architect can speak, but it has that virtue which Ruskin termed 'superabundance': it is at once a source of intellectual pleasure to the initiate and of sensuous delight to the layman. A fundamental concern with the relationship of public and private space to human scale is inherent in Classicism and in no other architectural tradition. That concern enhances the sheer beauty of mouldings and ornament which provide Classical buildings with layers of detail, enriching people's experience as they pause for second and third moments to appreciate the play of light on carved surfaces, the formalised naturalism of acanthus leaves, wreathes and garlands, the literary text of inscriptions, or the empathetic thrust of a column. Classicism – taken as a language of form – embraces all that richness, moreover it embodies it: it has it built in.

The teaching of architecture today is, I think, tragically haphazard. Students drown in the modishness of magazines and the faculty. In the absence of any structured pedagogy they lack any organisational tools with which to tackle a project. The only modern system of architectural education that succeeded in producing a large and diverse corps of skilful, confident and often inspired designers was the French academic method and it is time to consider emulating rather than merely nostalgising its achievements. Students should learn the grand tradition of Classicism with all its myriad permutations and its history of anti-Classical movements, including Modernism, through both historical research and investigative design.

It is neither an accident nor a testament to declining intelligence that so many of Modernism's finest achievements were those of its first generation. Le Corbusier grew out of the Classical tradition, even if his experience of it was largely provincial, and Mies and Gropius knew it cold. Their iconoclastic attitude towards Classical rhetoric was balanced by their profound knowledge of Classical systems of composition and proportion which disciplined their work no matter the expression. Modernism's success in dismantling the Classical system of education was suicidal; it reduced the rules of architectural composition and proportion to those of intuition and structural framing, condemning generations of students to a veritable Dark Age of ignorance.

Every form of learning is based on models – we cannot, indeed must not, expect each student to reinvent the discipline of architecture within a three-year programme of study or even within a full professional life. When I went to architecture school in the 1960s our models were not so much stylistic as individual: the heroes of contemporary architecture were our gods, either rising stars like Louis Kahn and Paul Rudolph or the established but still creative masters like Mies and Le Corbusier. Designing in the style of a particular architect was certainly better than basing one's work on the flow patterns of bubble diagrams and achieving only a diagram masquerading as a plan.

One architect does not a tradition make. A single person's *oeuvre* inevitably presents an interpretation too narrow and finite to sustain architecture's continued evolution; imitation of a hero quickly degenerates into parody. Kahn is the perfect exemplar of an architect working through tradition to achieve a personal interpretation of style. He was trained in the Classical tradition. Like most of his generation he rejected that tradition under the initial impact of Modernism and his early work was thoroughly banal. It was only when studying at the American Academy in Rome in 1949 that he was directly exposed to the panorama of Classicism, stretching from Antiquity past the Gothic interlude into the 1930s. The rest of his career represents an attempt to turn back, re-identify himself, and become a good architect through Classicism. I would rather see Mario Botta and countless other less gifted if sincere imitators of Kahn emulate that struggle to recapture the clarity and hierarchy of Classical composition than remain trapped in Kahn's much less convincing designs.

It is hardly restrictive or close-minded to suggest that we expose architectural education to years of history. Now that Modernism is dead as a creative force and it is fashionable to turn to the more distant past for inspiration, it behoves us to teach the past in a logical and structured way. If we do not, the creative energies of the present moment will have the same meteorically short career as those of Modernism. A new chapter in architectural history cannot sustain itself on a superficial understanding of the past or the faddish slickness of architectural magazines.

The Beaux-Arts method used precedent as a springboard for invention; and it taught precedent not only through classroom lectures but also first-hand through measuring and drawing buildings that were models of excellence. Most importantly, it required students to solve new problems with traditional styles. That is the only process by which an architect can truly begin to experience form, to comprehend its evolution, to accept it as data – and then to decide for himself whether, as such, it is to be copied, developed, eroded or discarded.

In our own day the rediscovery of Classicism has led Allan Greenberg to a scholarly 'correction' of prototypes; for Leon Krier it entails a romantic primitivism with revolutionary social implications. Throughout history Classicism has given order and form, composition and character to the most violently opposed concepts of architectural beauty. Whatever one's personal interpretation of the past, architecture must now go backwards in order to go forwards. As TS Eliot remarked, 'Art never improves, but the material of art is never quite the same.'[2]

The Renaissance cast its vision back beyond the Gothic to the presumed Golden Age of the ancients. Bramante and his colleagues measured the ruins of Rome, excavated and pillaged what they could, and debated the meaning of Vitruvius to recapture a lost theory of architecture. In the process Classicism evolved into a far more subtle, systematic and expressive language than their ancient ancestors would have thought possible. It became the language of modern times: the convincing expression of a man-centred secular culture. In 1876, American architects, glutted with the incoherencies and vulgarity of Victorian architecture, set out along the backroads of New England to document the fast vanishing vernacular and Georgian Classical buildings of the Colonial Era. Their research evolved into the Shingle Style, an ineffably American synthesis that referred to, yet transcended, its prototypes as it reflected its moment in time and defined an enduring typology. We are at such a turning point again, but it remains to be seen whether we turn to the past with the same acute critical vision that guided the Renaissance and the Ecole des Beaux-Arts. In 1923 Le Corbusier offered the challenge, 'architecture or revolution'. For our moment I would propose something different and more conciliatory: tradition *and* modernity.

Notes

1 This essay is a slightly revised version of an article which first appeared in *Precis 5*, The Journal of the Graduate School of Architecture and Planning, Columbia University, NYC, Fall 1984, pp 16-23. I wish to thank Gregory Gilmartin for his assistance in the preparation of this text which is in part based on a transcribed conversation with Daniel Monk and Jeffery Bucholtz, editors of *Precis 5*.

2 Quoted by Arthur Mizener, 'F Scott Fitzgerald 1896-1940. The Poet of Borrowed Time', in Alfred Kazin, ed, *F Scott Fitzgerald: The Man and His work*, Collier, New York, 1962, p 43.

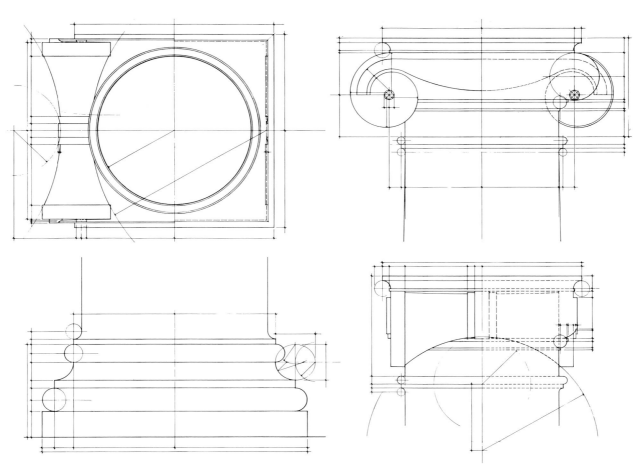

P 120 AND ABOVE: RESIDENCE IN HEWLETT HARBOUR, 1984-86

When I was asked to participate in the 'Post-Modernism and Beyond' symposium[1] I was surprised; at first glance so many of the others asked to take part seemed to be from the 'Beyond', a place from which I am surely not. But then I realised that Peter Eisenman, Frank Gehry, and I have everything in common especially when we are confronted with people, who in their zeal to make it clear that what we in our different ways do is wrong, lump us all together anyway. However, it is not my intention to criticise the critics.

Nor probably should it be to attempt once again to define the term 'Post-Modernism', yet such a redefinition seems to be needed, given that it has come to be so widely adapted and so carelessly applied. It is true that the term 'Post-Modernism', though an encompassing one, has by its very nature degenerated into a simple catch-all. In truth, the term is one that though broad is fairly precise, standing as it does for a complex set of values and beliefs that were initially articulated amidst a fairly precisely defined set of circumstances. While it may not have meant much to outsiders in the late 1970s, the term 'Post-Modernism' did mean a great deal to those who did the most to popularise it: to me and to Charles Jencks, and to Peter Eisenman, despite his subsequent, on-going critique of some of the ways its leading proponents have travelled. And it was a rebellious term – the rallying point for much-needed artistic change representing a profound reaction to a stultifying situation in architecture and the other arts. While each of us has gone our different ways, some even to the 'beyond', I would argue, we share the Post-Modernist experience. It was our liberation; and, try as some may to be free of the term, in each of our ways, I believe we are still Post-Modernists.

When 'Post-Modernism' was adopted as a term in the late 1970s, it already had behind it a certain history.[2] Arnold Toynbee had used the term in the 1950s and Joseph Hudnut, the rather under-appreciated Dean of the Harvard Graduate School of Design had used it right after the Second World War, as he struggled to articulate a locally appropriate approach to the European Modernism that was rather unquestioningly being adapted by American architects.[3] Hudnut hinted at a new synthesis, between European ideals and American circumstances; his suggestive ramblings seemed very intelligent to me in the late 1960s when I came upon his essay for the first time.

At the risk of repeating myself, I would like to try and describe the Post-Modernist ground that has helped guide me in my work as an architect. In 1977 I published a brief article, 'At the Edge of Post-Modernism,'[4] in which I attempted to put forward what I then believed and still believe to be the essential characteristics of the movement as a whole – its rejection of Modernism, and in particular late Modernism with its claims that an a-historical, non- or self-referential, essentially materialistic view of architecture was the exclusively appropriate position for contemporary architects. 'Post-Modernism,' I wrote,

> recognises that buildings are designed to mean something, that they are not hermetically sealed objects. Post-Modernism accepts diversity; it prefers hybrids to pure forms, it encourages multiple and simultaneous readings in its effort to heighten expressive content. Borrowing from forms and

strategies of both the Modern movement and the architecture that preceded it, it declares the past-ness of both. The layering of space characteristic of much Post-Modernist architecture finds its complement in the overlay of cultural and historical references in the elevations. For the Post-Modernist, 'More is More'.[5]

More than a decade later, I still believe in that definition; but while many observers continue to see Post-Modernism as just another of today's style-isms, I increasingly see it, and the work that since the mid 1970s has emerged in accord with its principles, as much more than that – as, in fact, nothing short of a balm that permits Modern architecture to heal the wrenching wound caused by Modernism. In making this claim, I use the term Modern, correctly I believe, as a broad term describing the post-Medieval era and I use a much less encompassing term – Modernism – to describe a movement within the Modern, a movement prevalent in the first half of the 20th century in architecture, the other plastic arts, and to a lesser extent in literature, a movement to create a self-referential, autonomous art, a movement that, for architects at least, is inherently contradictory given the public character of building. Given that Modernism, despite its claims to autonomy, relies on a critique of the Modern, even the most extreme proponents of its non- or self-referential approach such as Peter Eisenman, are Modern architects (and as I tried to argue in the essay 'Doubles of Post-Modern', Eisenman is in effect a kind of excessive contrary-minded Post-Modernist as well).[6] We are therefore all Moderns; but we are not all Modernists.

To be Modern is to have a sense of the past-ness of the past and to value, even idealise, various aspects of the past. Over time certain moments in history take on almost fixed values and come to be emulated, or at least referred to, as ideals. And in our work, our thinking, our discourse on architecture, we are all connected to a long tradition. For those of us operating in the West that tradition ultimately grows out of the Greco-Roman Classical world. Our Modern world and our way of working in the Modern world as architects, began in the late Medieval/early Renaissance period, when the Classical past was rediscovered in relationship to an emerging individuality of culture, language, which we call the vernacular. These terms, the Classical and the vernacular, are very important for me and I believe for any architect interested in locating contemporary work within the wider context of history and culture as well as within the physical context of a specific place. While taken as a whole the Classical is too complex to discuss in such a format as this, it is not, as some imagine, just a love of flowers on stone walls or ornamental systems, no matter how beautiful, that establishes Classicism's authority, though they surely contribute to it. Classicism's hold over all of us grows out of its much deeper values and our much deeper sense of loss.

The column is the principal element in the Classical language, symbolising at once both the erect human being and the tree. Grids of columns are like groves of trees; an analogy made even more explicit by ornamentation representing nature. The columns and lintels together with the secondary elements that constitute the orders are not only the grammar of the Classical language, not only a codified system of tectonic composition, but also a highly suggestive representational vocabulary that has the capacity to embrace, or should I say articulate, many meanings for the culture as a whole. Principally the Orders represent the human form in Nature. They have even been claimed to suggest gender.[7] A complex, visually engaging set of forms, the Classical Orders manage to distil, encapsulate, and communicate an archetypal concept of the natural and man-made world in a way that most people, even those without special education, can empathise with. Classicism succeeds because it is a language capable of infinitely complex permutations; its vocabulary is endlessly expressive and deepseated; it is abstract and real.

To talk of a 'vernacular' architecture or culture is to talk of one that grows up in a reasonably straightforward way out of a set of local conditions, solving problems of shelter and communication in a more or less non-self-conscious way: a vernacular grows out of a local soil that nourishes a local flavour; it offers simple solutions simply arrived at. A true vernacular is timeless in the very best sense of the word; it evolves but does not 'develop'. A vernacular architecture is a 'native' and a 'naive' architecture, one in which there is a common agreement about form. Building is added to building to create a coherent, nearly uniform environment encompassing the public and the private realms. Though traditional vernacular towns like Portofino near Genoa grew over a long time, they seem all of a piece because they are so natural to their place. This sense of inevitability has been increasingly held in high esteem in the Modern period as, increasingly, high cultures have become national, or even international, rather than local, synthetic rather than organic, individualistic rather than communal. The loss of the vernacular goes hand in hand with the growth of the Modern, as opposed to the Ancient or the Medieval culture, characterised as it is by the depersonalised, delocalised production of both goods and learning. As we have lost the vernacular we have come to value it all the more; to idealise it, to lift it to a status comparable to that of the Classical.

Palladio was in many ways the first 'Modern' architect, by bringing together, through misunderstanding and understanding, the two seemingly contradictory strains of building culture, the high Classicism of the Ancient World and the everyday vernacular of the local peasantry. Palladio juxtaposes but does not homogenise the high and the low; the ideal and the real. Palladio was the first to give lithic expression to the most important new social fact of the Modern era, the emergence of the middle class. Palladio's Villa Barbaro combines the simple directness of the vernacular, the local materials, the humble functional programme, with the middle class emphasis on individuality and its penchant for self-declaration. At Villa Barbaro, Palladio elevates the ordinary realm of the farm to that of the public realm of the town. Villa Barbaro is not just a house: it is a place and a proclamation. A farm building for a disfranchised urbanite, it is the exemplar of a new ideal: the suburban life, an ideal central to our experience to this day.

Palladio also misunderstood creatively, or just stupidly – I'm not sure – the meaning of the Roman temple which he took to be a model for the Roman house. By so doing he elevated the form of the single-family house to a hitherto unknown symbolic level; transforming ordinary shelter into an inhabited shrine consecrated to the family, to its material possessions, and to the place of the family in the larger order of things. In so doing Palladio combines the private and the public, the profane and the sacred, as never before.

In the early 19th century, when the mass-production of goods first became practical, the traditional vernacular was threatened as a means of production and as form-giver to the man-made landscape. As factories began to threaten the traditional life and physical structure of vernacular towns and villages, in keeping with the Modern tendency to idealise that which is lost, the vernacular was elevated to the level of an ideal, comparable to that of Classicism itself; it was assigned a moral value, that of

'honesty.' Craft was elevated into creed. To a surprising extent, as a result of this trend, the high architecture of the Medieval world has come to enjoy a status comparable to that of the Classical, as a kind of quintessential vernacular – but that is another point.

Now some would argue that the emergence of the machine in the early 19th century transformed both ordinary building and symbolic architecture, and indeed culture as a whole, bringing to birth a condition apart from the post-Medieval situation and, it is argued, one that puts the true beginning point of the Modern somewhere between the late 18th and the mid-19th century. Those who would so argue fail to see 19th and 20th-century architecture in a sufficiently broad perspective; they fail to understand the work of the recent past in relationship to the complex Modern matrix as a whole. The most destructive form of modernist exclusivity takes a fiercely materialistic view of architecture and adopts the Crystal Palace (Joseph Paxton, 1851) as emblematic of the break between the Renaissance tradition, to which they deny the term Modern, and Modernism to which they arrogate the term Modern. To see the realisation of the Crystal Palace in 1851 as the breaking point between the Renaissance tradition and what comes after is not only to rob the Modern of its early history and thereby its full meaning but also to confuse instrumentalities for instruments. Unquestionably, the Industrial Revolution had a profound effect not only on architecture but on all aspects of civilisation; so too did the emergence of mass democracy which began to take root in Western countries at about the same time. But though these twin phenomena profoundly altered the basic structure of the Modern condition, they were not a break with it; rather they were an outgrowth of it, a direct consequence of it even, heralding the full-fledged emergence of the secular world of the bourgeoisie. The Modernists, having elevated the craft vernacular to the level of an ideal, sought to create out of the machine and its processes a new vernacular. What was needed was a new synthesis, that would at once replace the faltering local craft vernacular with one based on the machine and would sustain the authority of the vernacular by virtue of association with the Classical. Instead Modernism sought to create a new, purely materialistic language of form. In trying to free architecture from all responsibility to traditional culture, to clear the way for a new world order of their own devising, Modernism lost sight of architecture's fundamental responsibilities. With Modernism, the horse sought to drive the cart.

As I see it, the Crystal Palace means just about the opposite of what the anti-traditionalist Modernists believed. Those who saw the messages of its form as the triumph of utility over symbol failed to look at the building very carefully. Close inspection will find that except for its use of new construction techniques, it is a very traditional building; it is in fact a grand Roman public building of the Imperial Era translated into glass, metal, and wood. It is a building that in every respect, starting with its name, is intended to represent inherited ideals and adapt them to modern conditions. In this sense, it is a Modern building in the full sense of that word, designed to be 'read' by the public in terms of prior experience. It is new, that is, up to date, and it is Modern. It is a palace, but a palace of glass. It is not an homogenisation of old and new, or an obliteration of the old in favour of the new; it is a balanced juxtaposition in the modern tradition of Palladio, that is why it is so aptly named – Crystal Palace!

Inside, the Crystal Palace reveals itself as not only a vast enclosure for the sake of sheltering a myriad of objects gathered together for public education, but also an internalisation of public life at unprecedented scale; it was the first building realised at the scale of mass democracy. It is Classical not because Paxton was not very good or very smart or very creative, nor because he had not been able to figure out how to erase away what he knew from the past, but simply because Paxton wasn't interested in creating a new language of architecture; such would not serve his purpose. His job was to say new things with the language architects already had, the language most people in his audience could understand. The use of the Classical enabled Paxton and his patron Prince Albert to establish connections with time-honoured, on-going values amidst the utter confusion of a plethora of objects that the machine made possible. This was exactly what Prince Albert had intended when he organised the display in the Crystal Palace. This great building, this Crystal Palace, reifies a set of traditional values in face of something new, it celebrates the new but does not succumb to it.

Mies van der Rohe is the critical architect of the Modern Movement. While it is clear now that Mies' attempt to invent an a-historical vocabulary of form and to combine it with a Classical grammar; in short to create a mechano-Classicism, was doomed, the cultural circumstances of its formulation were utterly logical. By the early 1900s many artists in the Western European tradition, particularly those in Northern Europe, felt that the Modern programme had run its course: that its architecture and urbanism was doomed only to repeat itself and no longer to clear new aesthetic ground. The tragic stalemate of World War One only served to confirm them in this belief, and the revolutionary politics that were evolved to bring the war to closure for a short time encouraged some few among these to claim a new millenium. In this context, Mies' post-war skyscraper projects were perfect; tectonically and formally convincing articulations of the Modernist programme applied to a new building type – the skyscraper – consecrated to the overthrow of the traditional urban order as it accommodated all the functional requirements of a new organisational elite.

Although Mies went further than any other architects in lifting the machine vernacular to the level of exalting architectural art, his work failed to replace that of traditional Classicism or the traditional vernacular in the public esteem. This is particularly so in England and even more so in the United States where the machine, the handmaiden of material progress that put these two nations on top of the economic heap, was seen by many as a negative force that was destroying not only the physical landscape but also the very social underpinnings of daily life. As a result, England and America have refused to mythologise the machine; for though they have enjoyed the benefits of industrialisation, they have seen first hand its terrible capacity for physical and psychological destruction. With no common history except the natural history of the continent, and no native architecture except that of the Amerindian, whose culture was disdained, the United States has experienced the conflict between the machine and the natural environment on an unprecedented scale. So it is not surprising that as Americans took hold of their continent and prospered, largely through the instrumentality of the machine, they did not turn to the machine for cultural sustenance but to its opposites, to nature and to the pre-industrial world; to natural history and architectural history. So it is that those Moderns who have had the longest-lived, most direct, intimate, and pervasive experience of the machine culture, the English and the Americans, those who were the first to have it and gained so much in material wealth from it, were also those who were most antipathetic to the Modernist programme and least willing to accept the argument that the brave new world of factory tectonics was superior to the traditional workshop world it replaced. To those who participated in the machine world on a day to day basis, architecture become increasingly sacred as an artefact of traditional culture, maybe even of myth. For the Anglo-American, architecture had to be much more than the 'bauen' beloved by Mies; architecture had to transcend materiality to become a symbolic cultural act.

If Mies' vision for the Modern was a noble failure; Jefferson's was a noble success. Jefferson saw architecture as the representation of ethical ideals, ideals which he believed essential for the success of the nascent American culture. Jefferson transferred these ideals, and the architectural forms which were their environ-

mental representation, to the American continent through a process of symbolic appropriation, one which has continued to characterise American culture to this day. The young Henry James commented on this and he offered what was perhaps the first and certainly the clearest articulation of this process, when in 1867 he wrote, 'I think that to be an American is an excellent preparation for culture. We have exquisite qualities as a race and it seems to me that we are ahead of the European races in the fact that more than any of them we can deal freely with forms of civilisation not our own, can pick and choose and assimilate and, in short, aesthetically . . . claim our property wherever we find it.'[8] Five years later, he commented a little more on the subject when he said 'it is a complex fate being an American, and one of the responsibilities that it entails is fighting against superstitious evaluation of Europe'.[9]

As I see it, it is distinctly different to be an American architect than to be a continental European architect, even to this day, and for this reason, the Post-Modernism that has emerged since the 1970s has come from America. As an architect I have seen as my mission to try to express, to represent, the values of American culture as I see them; not to impose values upon it. I'm fascinated more and more with Jefferson, of course, because he so brilliantly used architecture as a means of reflecting and influencing the direction of culture. Some say he was an amateur, a term used as a negative criticism. But I think amateurism is, in a sense, the highest way of doing things. As an amateur Jefferson understood that it was not the tectonic but the symbolic possibilities of architecture that were the first magnitude of importance. He used architecture as a part of a larger view of culture, not as a substitute for it. When he lived in Paris in the 1780s, he saw culture as a whole, he saw the new Classicism and distilled it, formed lessons, and brought them back. But the use he put them to, first at Monticello, and then at the University of Virginia, revealed him no mere copyist, nor even one engaged in a simple-minded act of transference, but a profound celebrant of architecture as an embodiment of human value across time.

At the University of Virginia, through a process of design and representation, Jefferson defined what American urbanism might be. He defined it by creating the great lawn, flanked by pavilions and the gardens and secondary pavilions behind, all combining to form what he called an academic village. No complex was an exact model for it; indeed there was no such planned idealised aggregation anywhere. Jefferson created a dream world so fundamental to the Modern condition of mass democracy that today it is correctly perceived as a type. He lined his village lawn with professors' houses, each of which confronted the greensward with a pedimented order from a Classical building of Antiquity so that the professors and the students could each study the Classical world, not only through books, not only through its verbal language, but through its architectural language or at least a pretty fair simulation of it. This was not done merely for the sake of an abstract learning, but so that the forms as well as the ideas of the Classical world would be taken up by the students after leaving the university. Jefferson capped his composition, not with a religious building, but with a library that is a half-scale version of the Pantheon in Rome. How significant was that functional transformation: in Jefferson's time the Roman Pantheon was a religious building, a Catholic church; and before that a building sacred to the Roman gods. Jefferson's Virginia Pantheon was a library. The choice of model seems very deliberate, rendering a point obvious by the transference of purpose and meaning from the realm of the spirit to the realm of the mind; in the new secular society, the building says, learning will be the new religion. So the building dedicated to education is an act of education as well; it is something that in satisfying a real need, elevates utility to the level of symbolic discourse.

Now the question arises; are buildings just sheds waiting to be decorated or nipped a bit here and tucked a bit there to give them a

127

'look' appropriate to a particular place or a particular programme? No, they are not – at least not quite. Every building is a unique undertaking; not just from the functional point of view, but also from its formal language. I believe that architecture cannot just be about programme or geometry. It must be more. Every architect must come to terms with that; but that 'more' must come from the circumstances outside the building itself. While some would say it can come from the architect's inner psyche, I would say that given architecture's public nature, it would better come from the context of the place, of the culture. Each new building has an obligation to comment on and contribute to the wider public realm. The place, its culture, and its physical history, as well as the requirements and the ideals of the client, all these are the text of architecture. If one is serious about this idea of building as public text, one cannot content oneself with the too easy task of seeing architecture as lithic autobiography.

In any case, though I sometimes write a book or the odd article in a journal, I don't think of myself as a theorist, but as an architect who tries to design buildings with some meanings attached. And I would like to conclude with that in mind, to try to discuss the work, or the meanings, in the hopes of answering at least some of the questions you might have, and in so doing revealing one, but by no means the only way, to formulate and fulfil a Post-Modernist approach. So I would conclude by discussing a building my colleagues and I have recently completed, one which illuminates the possibilities inherent in the story-telling approach I mentioned earlier and, as well, casts light on the complex circumstances that both distance and connect modern American architecture from that of the Western European tradition as a whole.

The Mexx building Voorschoten, Netherlands (1985-1987), brought to my mind many of the issues that I have tried to raise in here: in particular, the distinction between the American and European perceptions of Modernism. Our clients, a company designing and manufacturing high-style, street-wise clothing for the young and hip, acquired a landmark building of the 1850s that had been built as a silversmith's factory and was now derelict. Redesigned, and doubled in size, it now serves as our client's business headquarters and design centre. Working in Holland as an architect, not visiting as a tourist, forced me to come to grips directly with a dilemma that was surely central to the incandescent Dutch Modernism of the early part of this century: the sense of aesthetic and environmental completeness that one gets wandering through cities like Amsterdam or Delft. American architects have never had this problem. We are lucky if we have three blocks of anything consistent and fine. Though giving rise to pleasurable sensations, such completeness also creates anxieties for the architect. What to do in a built world that seems so perfect and complete? Surely if I were an architect raised in such an environment, as say Mies or Rietveld were, it would drive me nuts. It surely would have a seriously inhibiting influence. In our individualistic age, such an environment seems to give rise not to the question 'what can a single architect contribute', but to one that is ultimately destructive, 'what can an architect do to it?'

The question was the same for me as I contemplated so much that was fine and finished. But my response was distinctly different. For me the challenge was one of evolution not revolution. To develop my approach I first turned to history in order to better understand the situation in Holland. In the early part of this century, Modernism in Holland took two distinct directions: the abstract formulation of De Stijl and the expressive functionalism of Constructivism. De Stijl was painterly; Constructivism was tectonic. Gerrit Rietveld's Schroeder House (1924) was the quintessential work of the De Stijl, like a painting one can walk through. But bring your own hammer, screwdriver, and paint brush because it is always falling apart when you are there! It always needs a little fixing up. It is not at all about 'bauen'. But it is not about the public

realm either – it totally contradicts the environment around it as it defies the very materiality of construction itself. It is an art object placed in the town; it is not a building in the conventional sense of the term, but a construct that uses the excuse of habitation to make a statement about pure aesthetics, albeit a very powerful one, a brilliant one, one that gives me much pleasure, but one that is not, in the most fundamental sense, architectural.

JA Brinkman and LC Van der Vlugt's Van Nelle factory (1927-1930), designed with Mart Stam is, on the other hand, a great building as building, one deeply rooted in machine inspired tectonics as it is entranced by the assembly line processes that it is conceived to accommodate. While the aesthetic effects of the Schroeder House are precisely calculated, those of the Van Nelle seem to have been arrived at more freely; it is a building that overflows with exuberance, wit even. It seems full of activity, of life, celebrating not only the new building technology, or the production processes that are its *raison d'être*, but also the pleasure it brings to the workers, bathed in natural light. The particularities of the programme, rather than a self-conscious aesthetic, are the inspiration for the design, so full of life with its chutes stretching across voids, its conning-tower tearoom, its easy volumetric juxtapositions. True, as a self-contained large scale industrial complex, it does not have to take on the issue of local context. So it is not fair to make too much of it in contrast to Schroeder but the differences are there to make for points of comparison.

In any case, the building we put together for Mexx restores the old and creates something new, but something that seeks to grow out of the liberating Constructivism of Van Nelle rather than the hot-house aesthetics of Schroeder. Ours is, in a way, an effort to establish the lost history of the original building, which like the company that built it, stagnated in early 20th century. We restored the exterior of the old building, but its ground floor interiors, probably never much to begin with, and ruined when we found them, were reconfigured for use as an executive suite, with ceilings shaped to coddle the precious Dutch light. Design studios were located above in the attic-like spaces on the second floor. As one moves from the old building to the new, the transition is not abrupt but gradual as if the building had a 'natural' history.

To make it clear that this 'history' was consciously evolved, fragments of the walls of the original were reproduced as detached elements framing the outdoor courtyard suggesting the interweaving of aesthetics across time, as if a much larger traditional building had been partially demolished to introduce such environmental benefits of the 20th century as superabundant natural light and intimacy between inside and out. But the 'new' elements are intended to be distinctly Dutch, incorporating the free curves and joyous mechano-morphology that I admire at Van Nelle and in the work of the engineer-architect Sybold van Ravestyn. So, although Mexx may seem at first glance out of keeping with my recent work, or at least my work in America, the ideas that influenced its shaping are not; it is a building about other buildings and about its place in its landscape and in its culture. If it succeeds as architecture, it does so because it is a building that gives environmental and cultural pleasure, not merely as abstract composition or form, but as a representation of shared experience and shared values; it builds upon the past, drawing Modernism into the wider family of the Modern.

The problem has been the same for me since I started to practice, working in the studio space that had been created on the top floor of Louis Kahn's Yale Art Gallery. Out the window lay before me Yale's skyline with its wonderful, Gothic-style buildings, widely admired by 'real' people, but condemned by architects as irrelevant expressions of a somewhat laughable past. For me, these wonderful structural/conceptual hybrids, dismissed as 'girder Gothic', exerted a strong pull away from the direction of contemporary work. Despite teachers and many of my fellow students who said 'You can't do those any more', I began to wonder about the events that had caused architecture to so change in the 20 years between the time the last of those Yale buildings had been built and the time when I enrolled as a student. My book on George Howe begun while still a student at Yale, but not published until 15 years later, was a direct product of my curiosity about this revolution in taste.[10] Economic depression, world war and a sense of cultural inferiority had all combined to rob American and most other Western architects of the courage to continue their dialogue with the past. It was not only better to 'make it new',[11] to use Ezra Pound's phrase, it was essential. The world, I was told, had so dramatically changed, that only little flat roofed boxes could do; and that modern architecture could only be defined as buildings your mother and practically everyone else hated. In order to be good, one had to be hated.

Deep down, I never wanted to be that different; I wanted to be an architect who made things better, not different, or at least not different merely for the sake of being different. But it took quite a while to be the architect I wanted to be, rather than the one prevailing taste said I should be. First Vincent Scully and then Paul Rudolph and then Robert Venturi taught me how to look at the buildings of the past, and in those buildings I saw something that I could not see in the work of my own time, something that I thought worth holding on to, something that had values the 'new' did not have on its own. So I tried to make buildings that are old and new.

Architecture is at its best, it seems to me, when it digs deep into culture in order to affirm, and sometimes even to re-establish, values and ideals. It is not enough for buildings to express the architect's tortured soul or psyche, or the painstaking processes of design that lead to the final product, or some abstruse literary theory or compositional game. This is not to say that the house of Architecture is not big enough to include those things. But at its most basic, architecture must be the reification of public values. A building must be a public act of communication: a coherent presentation, representation, reification, not merely of programme, function, or conventions belonging to the discipline itself, but also of the things that belong to the world outside which it must serve, honour, and depict. It must be in its essence a portrait of places, of cultures, of beliefs and of dreams. Architecture must be more than the lithic representation of the private fantasies or inner demons of the architect. It is not the built version/illustration of a written text. Architecture is the most public of all the arts. The most obdurate of the arts. It is also the least personal of the arts. It is not at its best when it is pursued as an instrument of radical change. This is not to say that it cannot contribute to society's gradual evolution, but that its ways are more conservative. It must comprehend the meaning of the past in order to move on.

And so I could reaffirm if not for you, at least for myself, that the task of architecture is not to represent a collapse of values or the crisis of our times. What time in history has not had a crisis? Or at least thought that it did not? So I would reaffirm for myself that it is not appropriate for the architect to arrogate to himself the self-delusory belief that he can give form to the spirit of his own time. Every architect, if he has a bigger idea than just simply getting the job and building the building, must have a sense of larger purpose. But that purpose seems to most properly lie in the realm of narrative rather than autobiography, representation rather than illustration. The architect may best be suited to represent what he sees and what he knows from what is around him, and to use what he sees and knows from what is around him, as well as what he knows from the past to give new work resonance.

I believe architecture is a story-telling art, a narrative. The story I seek to tell is that of America, or more precisely what it means to be an American, whether an American in America or an American abroad. Architecture has played a special role in the continuous struggle of Americans to define who they are, given the vast emptiness of our continent, and our shared experience as aliens all, we search for a collective identity. As we face the challenge of creating a history and culture for ourselves, we necessarily appropriate past forms and symbols, raising them to mythic proportions. If we are any good at what we do, we also make them our own.

Notes

1   This essay is a revised version of a talk delievered at the 'Post-Modernism and Beyond' Symposium, University of California, Irvine, October 27, 1989.

2   For a discussion of the varieties of Post-Modernism see my essay 'Doubles of Post-Modern', *Harvard Architectural Review*, 1, Spring 1980: 74-87.

3   The term seems to have been initiated by Joseph Hudnut in his essay 'The Post-Modern House', *Architectural Record* 97, May 1945: 70-75, which was re-printed as chapter 9 in Hudnut's *Architecture and the Spirit of Man*: Harvard University Press, Cambridge, Massachusetts, 1949, 109-119. Its earliest influential use was in Arnold J Toynbee's *A Study of History*, 8: Oxford University Press, New York, 1954-1959, 338.

4   Robert AM Stern, 'At the Edge of Post-Modernism: Some Methods, Paradigms and Principles for Architecture at the End of the Modern Movement,' *Architectural Design* 47, April 1977: 274-286.

5   Robert AM Stern, 'At the Edge of Post-Modernism,' *op cit*, p. 286.

6   Robert AM Stern, 'Doubles of Post-Modern', 66.

7   For an extensive discussion of the origin of the orders, including the gender issue, see George Hersey, *The Lost Meaning of Classical Architecture*: The MIT Press, Cambridge, Massachusetts 1988, 33-36.

8   Letter, Henry James to Thomas Sergeant Perry, September 20, 1867, quoted in Leon Edel, ed, *Henry James Letters*, Vol 1: The Beknap Press of Harvard University Press, Cambridge, Massachusetts, 1974, 77.

9   Letter, Henry James to Charles Eliot Norton, Febuary 4, 1872, quoted in Leon Edel, *op cit*, 274.

10   Robert AM Stern, *George Howe: Toward a Modern American Architecture*: Yale University Press, New Haven, 1975.

11   Ezra Pound, *Make It New: Essays*: Faber & Faber, London, 1934.

P 124 AND ABOVE: MEXX INTERNATIONAL HEADQUARTERS, THE NETHERLANDS, 1985-87

CHARLES JENCKS
A DIALOGUE WITH ROBERT AM STERN

Four Contributions to Architectural Culture
– I see three main areas of your contribution to architectural culture in general: architecture, writing and teaching. There is a fourth possibility – Stern as the catalyst with the 'Greys' in the 60s and the Architectural League in such shows as 'Forty under Forty'. Would you agree that those are your three, perhaps, four areas of contribution, or do you see a fifth?
I don't see a fifth. No, four is pretty good.
– Would you agree with my order: architecture first, writing second, teaching third and then being a catalyst fourth?
Well, it's OK until you get to teaching versus catalyst. I often wonder after a day in the Columbia studio: what have I actually done or accomplished? Many of the people who work for me or with me and others who take up important positions in other people's offices are people who were my students; so I would say that I have had some influence as a teacher, but much more so, I think, as an architect of course, and as a writer, and with the television programme, 'Pride of Place', as something of a public spokesman for architecture. Although the critics had their way with me, the public continues to respond to the television series. I get letters and people stop me in the street so I know it had a tremendous impact and continues to count. That is an extension of writing I suppose.
– So you would see a fifth contribution as TV?
Well, not as a steady diet.
– The only architect I know with a comparable range is Kisho Kurokawa who actually had a weekly television programme, has written over 30 books and has an architectural office of over 100 people.
I am not in that league.
– No, but you have combined in a synergetic way at least three, possibly four, different professions and they overlap rather than conflict. Teaching, for instance, has fed your offices and your office probably feeds Columbia University. Do you have some people who go back and teach?
For the first time one of my associates is teaching with me. I have been fairly selfish about this, saying that if I give up three afternoons and a couple of mornings a week, that is a big enough contribution to the University; that I can't run an office with people running off and teaching as well. Now that I'm sharing the teaching with an office associate, I'm at the university less and a close collaborator is getting some teaching experience which he likes.
– Another aspect of this is that you are a fountainhead for a lot of other offices, and I'll mention a comparison which you will find immensely flattering: Norman Shaw, in England, who was the guiding light for the London School in about 1880. Do you think your work and teaching has galvanised a group of people around New York and Massachusetts who come out of your office? Is there a Scuola di Sterno?
There are a number of employees and associates who have made important contributions in this office who now have independent offices. The top people in the office seldom leave to work for another office; it is usually to set up on their own. There are people like Gavin Macrae Gibson, Peter Pennoyer, Charles Warren and John Ike, to name four, who were first students of mine, and then

associated with the office; all of whom have established independent practices and each of whom I think will make a contribution. So far their work seems to be expanding and interpreting ideas we shared together in this office.
I pride myself on having warm, collegial relationships with a lot of architects. Most go only a bit beyond the social, but others achieve a considerable level of artistic and intellectual discourse. A few are wonderfully improbable – my friendship with Peter Eisenman for example, who by the very oppositeness of his nature from mine and his point of view from mine is my perfect alter-ego: 'If I didn't invent Peter Eisenman who would have?' Stanley Tigerman is a close friend from Yale days who, depending on which of his 'lives' he's living is someone I share ideas with or spar with over differences. And then there are others like Robert Kliment, Frances Halsband, Taft, Peter DeBrettville, who share ideas. We dine and talk about things from time to time, so that is all very nice. My favourite architects are what I would like to be: multidimensional, multivalent.

Eclecticism: The Vernacular of a global city
– The 'multidimensional' is a nice swerve because it brings up the 'One Dimensional Man', the 'one dimensional' architect. All this variety and multidimensionality means you are more pluralist than the usual architect. I would say that you are the ultimate cosmopolite architect and like a good cosmopolite you are an extension of the world's implosion of different cultures. So if you like, eclecticism is a mirror image of pluralisation in our culture.
Eclecticism is such a loaded term. If by eclectic you mean that I seize upon different directions, or ideas, or architectural vocabularies, so be it. That is true and I relish it. But I don't like to think of myself as an eclectic who wakes up in the morning and says 'Ah today the Greek' or 'today Gothic' just for the sake of it. I am always interested in the freest possible explorations of form but always these explorations must be undertaken in relationship to what I deem programmatically and culturally and contextually appropriate.
– You're distinguishing between what I called 'radical' and 'weak' eclecticism, an eclecticism that is motivated more than it is whimsical.
I try to motivate the forms.
– I accept that, but my question is to do with the forces within our culture and the global city; the fact that you are responding to forces that are out there. You have to relate to 10 different clients with 10 different tastes and 10 different cultural situations. The cosmopolite takes the philosophical position that the world does not have a single language, so it is morally correct to vary the style. It is a responsibility.
– So having a single style would be immoral to a cosmopolite.

Four Periods and Styles
– I want to periodise your work into three or perhaps four stages. The 'First Bob' is early Venturi, a period from 1965 to 1975, in which you were an eclectic Post-Modernist who was really interested in spatial developments. This preoccupation continues throughout your work, but there is an identifiable mode where you

131

are consciously a follower of Venturi, like Borromini was a follower of Bernini. You never fought with Venturi, as far as I know.

Relations these days are, shall we say, quiescent? But we never fought: why should we? We have too much to share and too much to do.

– Bernini wanted to assassinate Borromini, get rid of him.

You'll have to ask Venturi.

– It seems to me that one of your best buildings from this period is the Lang House, which has a wonderful space and witty self-consciousness that perhaps Venturi himself couldn't quite bring himself to do ... You have felt freer than any other architect today to admit influences.

Well I more than admit an influence from Venturi. I see one of my important contributions to architecture as my early recognition of his ideas and my proselytisation of same. Venturi's early buildings, his cultural vision of architecture, and his often very incisive analysis of historical and contemporary form, pointed me in the direction I've taken as no other architect or teacher did. Others [who influenced me] are Charles Moore and, later, Michael Graves, particularly after he had his Saul-Paul conversion to Post-Modernism. Sometimes James Stirling inspires me a lot, and now I'm even beginning to see things in Frank Gehry's work that I wish I'd done (by the way, Frank Gehry is one of those architects whose friendship and ideas I value even if we are sometimes worlds apart in our work). Philip Johnson has always been an exemplar for me: as a designer and even more importantly as someone who sees architecture as something of real importance. I have always been in awe of his intelligence – his ability to seize upon ideas and put them to work in conversation and in his own practice; on the other hand, he can be incredibly contrary ... but never dull and never less than a brilliant mind. Beyond this, I cannot think of anyone amongst the living. But in the past there are many many. Given my predisposition as a cosmopolite (which is your phrase), I see past architects as essentially present. In a funny way I view architecture in completely a-historical terms. Certainly I am in no way interested in the historicist, 'spirit of the times' obsessions of the Modernists. Lutyens may be in the grave, but his buildings are still very much with me to be analysed, and his ideas to be debated as if they had just been published in *Progressive Architecture*. I have the same feeling when I go to Rome and look at Borromini – I am still fighting out that battle between Borromini and Bernini in my mind, as though it were happening today. I am interested in history as such, but I am really interested in historical buildings, both because they are wonderful, and because they are all here together with me in the present.

– Do you accept this characterisation of the period 1965-75 as the 'First Bob'?

The 'First Bob' was a cocky kid who had a bit of work, who had a bit of ability to express himself with words and who was in New York at an interesting time when change was in the air. I have the immodest willingness to say I helped to initiate a very interesting period in our architecture. This sense that individuals can influence events comes from having been at Yale at a time when Paul Rudolph and Vincent Scully stressed the power of the individual creative act. I was tremendously influenced by Scully, and by Rudolph, even though Rudolph and my forms are as different as his prejudice against historical reference is from my affinity for it. What is always behind me, is Rudolph's sense that a successful building must come alive three-dimensionally.

– Now the 'Second Bob' dates from 1975 to 1982 – please feel free to reshape these dates.

I guess this is the period between the two Biennales – between 1976 and 1980 – so 1975 is a good date. With the publication of the Lang House, the 'White and Grey' event and the 'Five on Five' essays, I had established a position. 1975 also marked my entrance

into the international arena; I began preparing for the Venice Biennale of 1976, which was an important event. First of all, a number of Americans, myself, Eisenman, Hejduk, Ambasz, Tigerman and others were asked to participate in that international forum. Second, in part as a result of my suggestion, the Americans agreed to turn their attention to the problem of the suburbs, an issue that would help us to define ourselves as a group distinct from the mega-scale-minded Europeans invited to exhibit as well (Herzberger and Kroll are two of these that now come to mind ...). I saw this as an opportunity to relate the individual houses which were my stock-in-trade, to more complex issues of urbanism which I had not focused on since my stint as an architect for the New York City government in the late 1960s.

– That's when you consolidate the interest in suburban as against the usual urban situations, and also when you start producing a lot of Shingle Style designs. You evolve from Freestyle to the Edwardian Shingle Style, following Norman Shaw's development from Queen Anne Revival to Edwardian Baroque. It's almost a parallel, would you agree?

My knowledge of Shaw's work is pretty good, and I don't disagree. There was a general tendency in American architecture at the same time, if you look at, say, McKim, Mead and White's move from an American version of the Queen Anne Style to a more traditional, continental Classicism. It was an impulse in English/American architecture which had an enormous number of parallels to my own feelings. I live in the past, and in the future, and in the present: it is very complicated every day when I get up.

– Philip Johnson put down Frank Lloyd Wright by saying, in the early 1930s, that he was the 'greatest architect of the 19th century'.

I think you've got this wrong. In the early 1930s he thought Wright was dead – or at least finished as a creative force. But when Wright not only proved to be alive but also at the peak of his artistic powers, Johnson revised his assessment and claimed him as our greatest architect or, as he put it, our greatest 19th-century architect, leaving room for Mies.

– What about someone saying 'you are the greatest architect of the Edwardian period'? What would you say if Peter Eisenman said that?

I wouldn't be insulted to be the greatest anything ... and it's flattering to be associated with the Edwardian period. It was an age of confidence and an age of high style and high social responsibility – a wonderful mix – people don't recognise that. Its reforms and artefacts interest me: the work of Lutyens, Belcher and Joass, Halsey Ricardo, Charles Holden, the wonderful early housing projects of the London County Council – all these I like. Hampstead Garden Suburb was not built for the rich, but for the poor, and Lutyens and Parker and Unwin all worked on it.

– You're coming across as having a social conscience – 'building for the poor'.

Don't forget that after architecture school, a year at the Architectural League, and a short time in Richard Meier's office, I went on to spend more than two years in city government. It was an important moment for American architects with what you call a 'social conscience': when the '60s' spirit was in the ascendancy. I was one of a handful of architects who were inspired by John Lindsay – New York's reform mayor – to become involved in the politics of housing and planning in New York. I worked for Lindsay in his mayoral campaign in 1965, served on his Task Force on Urban Design from 1966-67 and later joined the city's newly constructed Housing and Development Administration.

– What years were they?

1967-1969, and in the early 70s as a consultant.

– I see your social conscience coming out of an interest in suburbia, but this sounds to me like Richard Meier talking about his social conscience.

I try not to wear my social conscience on my sleeve.

– But nor do you wear it the way the London County Council wore it: in building social housing projects. You may have thought about it, but how many have you built?

How many have any American architects been able to build over the past 15 years?

– At least Richard Meier, who wants to be known for his social conscience, had the Twin Parks social housing in the Bronx.

Richard built Twin Parks at a time when I was working for the city. He is older than I am and much longer established. But Meier's project was built within a framework of ideas and policies that I, along with Jaquelin Robertson, Alex Cooper, Richard Weinstein, Jon Barnett and others, helped formulate, legislate and implement.

– Then I ask, is your social conscience frustrated? Or stillborn?

Frustrated. But your line of questioning is too simple-minded. Let me put it this way: 'social conscience' isn't the right phrase. It smacks too much of what Robert Moses derided as the 'goo-goo-isms' of the do-gooder; it's patronising and condescending. I have always been interested in how people live in cities or wherever they gather in groups. Through my writings, and occasional theoretical projects like Subway Suburb, I have explored one manifestation of this issue in detail. Though I have not yet realised any major urban projects, I did win the competition for 'social' housing on Roosevelt Island in 1975 with a very strong and very controversial scheme; so controversial, in fact, that the jury, chaired by José Sert, split and awarded three other first prizes to Sert look-alike solutions. None of these schemes were built owing to the financial collapse of the sponsoring agency (the New York State Urban Development Corporation) and the subsequent retreat of the federal government from subsidised housing construction. So I feel frustrated about my ability to realise my ideas; but I nonetheless feel that I have made a contribution to the philosophy of social housing and inner-city urbanism. Of course now I have plenty of work, yet there is no real opportunity for social housing – except one small project at Tegel, Berlin as part of Charles Moore's master plan. But I've used the suburbs and the speculative house for the affluent as a testing ground for ideas which could also be explored for the poor. The Subway Suburb project posed the problem of rebuilding Brownsville and East New York. I later took the idea up with students at Yale and Columbia, focusing on the famous wasteland of Charlotte Street in the South Bronx. I am extremely serious about the problem – I consider mass housing a part of my responsibility to the city as a whole. But I want to make it clear that I am interested in social problems as they influence architecture – not just do-gooderness. Architecture is not built sociology or social reform . . . And I do not think that 'housing' is a sub-set or sub-style of architecture. The great housing has been part of architecture as such, whether by Lutyens at Page Street, or Le Corbusier in his early proposals in Paris.

– The 'Third Bob', from 1982 to the present, makes a shift to the Classical Revival interpreted in a broad sense. It is a revival rather than Free-Style Classicism, which is what I was writing about at the time. There is your Kentucky Farmhouse which is slightly Neo-Classical. There is the New Jersey Villa, which we know is a mixture of Charles Platt and Spanish/Italian work. There is also the Vero Beach housing, influenced by Addison Mizer, Hewlett Harbour influenced by Soane's Pitzhanger and Cockerill's Ashmolean. Would you agree that there is a development?

It is a widening of vocabulary. But it is not Classical Revival as a supervening direction; I am not much more interested in a Classical Revival as you seem to use the term, than I am in a 'Spiritual Revival'. I am not a convert on a crusade, nor am I interested in the past as a closed set of formal inventions that should be reiterated as gospel. I have turned to Classical themes as a logical extension of my culturally and physically inspired contextualism. For contextual reasons, the Kentucky Farmhouse could not have been a shingled cottage, whereas in Long Island that would have made utterly good sense. All the other houses you have mentioned are in communities in which shingled cottages would not be appropriate . . . So I broadened my design vocabulary in order to better address issues of character and places as I saw them.

– But if I look at your work statistically from about 1982 on, the emphasis shifts, as you start to investigate the Classical. You become pulled in by the demands of your clients and by the new interests in Classicism.

All of those things are absolutely true. My interest in Lutyens was my way into Classicism. Lutyens also began with vernacular-inspired houses. He extended his vocabulary to include High Classicism – but he did so in relation to cultural issues and not only for the pleasure of the artistic challenge. To the end of his long career he worked with a wide variety of form languages, high and low alike, frequently combining them to make a point. My interest in Lutyens goes back to when I was at Yale: we discussed Lutyens in a graduate art history seminar I took with Vincent Scully in 1962 or 1963.

– Really, before Venturi wrote about 'Learning from Lutyens'?

Well, I can't remember for sure, but I had read an early draft of Venturi's book, *Complexity and Contradiction*, at about that time so he may have been the stimulus for my further investigations of Lutyens. I should also mention architects who could not have but helped to inspire me in my growing interest in Classicism. Leon Krier's categoric statements were so thrilling, riddled as they are with contradiction: make a jet plane ride half way across the world to give a lecture by candlelight – what a magnificent contradiction. Absolutely. And when I went to see Bofill's work as I was helping to organise the Strada Novissima for the Biennale in 1980, my eyes opened further to the possibilities of a contemporary monumental Classicism in the public realm. Beyond a primitive level of chronology I don't care about who did what first. What is important is the sharing of an idea or an ideal and what an architect does with his beliefs – the work that is. But then someone comes along like a Krier, or a Greenberg, and it seems as if you must push in those directions, to try the extremes. That's the trigger for me.

– Let me give you a negative version of this from your enemies.

I don't have enemies.

– Just friends who misunderstand you? You know that Philip Johnson used to be called in Britain 'the most sincerely hated living architect', until you took that role from him.

I guess if I live long enough someone even more evil – or is it honest? – than Philip or me will come along to take the place of honour.

– If you look at the 'Third Bob' there is a way in which he shifts to the Classical Revival and gets caught in the Era of Reagan. How do you wear the neo-conservative label?

I think of myself as 'radically conservative'.

– How do you distinguish yourself from the Reaganites?

I am not very political.

– That is what Philip Johnson says – a dangerous remark for a neo-conservative.

'Liberalism', 'conservatism' – these terms are so misused . . . so abused, nowhere more so than in the corridors of the University.

– Are you more sympathetic to Allan Bloom?

I haven't read Allan Bloom, but from what I have read about his work, I guess I am sympathetic.

– Who do you find affinity with on a political or philosophical level?

You are pushing me into an area in which I don't want to be.

– At certain points in life one has to face these questions . . .

Maybe I haven't reached this point yet. I am, and I think every architect is, a conservative. To build is to establish. In the same sense that you are conserving values, you reaffirm values. Too bad so many architects delude themselves into believing that they are *not* conservative – it makes for such pretentious lectures and magazine articles.

– You know that Frank Lloyd Wright's first essay was called In The Cause Conservative *for precisely that reason?*

I am in that sense a conservative. You remember my article *The Doubles of Post-Modern*, in which I aligned myself with people like TS Eliot and others who want the new but not at the expense of the old. I am a modern; but I think there is a vast difference between the obsessional zealousness of Modernism and the subtle complexities of modernity.

– Remember that TS Eliot ended, as he said 'a Royalist in politics, a Classicist in literature and an Anglican in religion'.

I am still an American, not very religious . . .

– If you were British would you be a royalist?

Sure, if I were British I'd be a royalist in the framework of the constitutional monarchy. But that doesn't mean I'd not be a democrat. Does this make sense?

– Did you vote for Reagan?

I am embarrassed to say I don't usually vote, not out of principle but out of lassitude; but I did vote in the last election. I was going to vote for George Bush, but my son, who is now 21, told me that if I voted for Bush 'that was the end'. I knew Bush was going to win whether I voted for him or not, so I voted for Dukakis, and I regretted it every minute of the day I pulled the lever, and still do. I made the correct family decision, but not a very good political one.

– These tensions you are revealing appear in your work. The basic one is the opposition between Modernism and Classicism. The 'Third Bob' appears to have left the Venturian irony, the 'First Bob'.

I don't think I have departed; but that I've built upon it. Also, I see the tension as one between Modernism and Traditionalism, not merely Classicism. The first book by Venturi is filled with the ironies of culturally compromised form. It is not like the second book on Las Vegas, which is where he gets into trouble for me. That is where we part. The first book – with its complexities and ironies, is to me a valid critique of the then architecture, and it's a valid guide – a way out of a dead end.

– I don't want to put words into your mouth, but they are your own: they come from the oxymoron of your book Modern Classicism. *There is an agenda within Modernism which is opposed to Classicism. They are also opposed in your character, but often you sublimate opposition. Or make it disappear. Sometimes you smooth over the differences, and act and build as if they didn't exist.*

Or resolve it. Remember in the first few pages of *Modern Classicism* I point out that there needs to be a written companion volume dealing with the vernacular styles, one which might be called *Modern Naturalism*. Taken together they define the *Modern Traditional* approach. Henry-Russell Hitchcock tried to define early 20th-century-architecture along these lines in his book *Modern Architecture: Romanticism and Reintegration* (1929), which more than any other book on the history of the Modern in the 19th and 20th centuries continues to impress me.

Disney Casting Center: Pastiche, Irony and Taste

– Let's look at another aspect. In the Disney Casting Center there is a way in which, as in Venturi's work, you are doing a Pop pastiche. There are, for example, elements of the Doge's Palace – why?

The Casting Building houses a 'back-office' function on an extremely prominent, 'front-office' site. It is, in fact, the only building representing Disney that faces the Interstate highway. It was put there to encourage people to work for Disney. It was my task to house various employment-related functions and to transform what would otherwise be a low-budget office building into an expression of Disney's 'magic', 'sense of fun' – its corporate persona.

I based the building on the Doge's Palace because it is so familiar an architectural icon, in the films and even more so in the theme parks. Disney uses Venetian themes prominently because they work so well in the Florida landscape (we originally planned to visually 'float' the building in water, but the hydrology was not as cooperative as I'd initially been led to believe). Venice is an extraordinary place, an intersection between the East and West, North and South – it is a model for the techniques and collage juxtapositions that Disney so brilliantly explores in the Magic Kingdom and Epcot. The relationship between buildings, water and land in Venice is a perfect analogy to what we wanted to achieve.

– You pastiche it by expanding that diagonal diaper pattern and amplifying the scale, like Lutyens does in his mass-housing in London. Then you have 12 gilt statues which line this indoctrination hall. You go down a long walkway when you are trying to become a member of the Disney Corporation, past the statues in the passage, past the Mickey Mouse iconography, and then arrive at a small hall. It is rather intimidating – it's a very long way to the reception hall.

Yes, except that when there are 100 people standing in line waiting to get to the receptionist, it is much nicer standing indoors in the air-conditioned space, bathed in natural light that floods in from above, engulfed, and entertained by the Disney iconography on the left and the right.

– Is this not a perfect turning back on itself of the Disney ideology? There is no irony or consciousness here, you are a perfect handmaiden for the Disney Corporation. The whole point of irony in Post-Modernism is to allow for dissent: to give a double reading, to build for the corporation while at the same time suggesting an alternative value system. You see what I am driving at?

No, I don't see what you are driving at, so I can't answer your question. I would like to offer an observation that Bob Venturi made in a meeting that was held with a number of architects who share Disney as a client. He said that Disney's is the only 20th-century iconography that is virtually universal.

– But it is an iconography without meaning. It is the perfect meaningless symbol, because it entails no commitment. When you believe in Mickey Mouse you believe in nothing.

I'm not so sure. I think you believe in decency. When you believe in Snow White you believe in something: optimism.

– No you don't, it is very corporate, it is an ersatz symbol system. It's close to 1984 *and* Brave New World, *whose corporate control is actually pleasurable for those being controlled. You are not going to overcome this problem.*

I think it is a problem that you have, and I don't have.

– It is a problem of our culture, it is neither you nor I.

I can believe in Mickey Mouse and Voltaire and Jefferson and others – I can hold contradictory ideas in balance. Why can't you? My sense that there is no one 'right way' goes back to my earliest experience in the architectural arena – way back when you were in your social relevance days at Harvard, editing *Connection* and when, with a rather different purpose in mind, I was editing *Perspecta* at Yale. Remember it was I who commissioned the article in which Charles Moore argued in defence of Disneyland's architecture and urbanism as something that filled a void in the post-war American city.

– But Charles Moore knows that no one can dissent from Disney World, that everyone is made over in the Disney Image.

But I don't find Disney quite so tyrannical as you, nor as evil as you imply. In fact, it is a kind of secular church, like the movies – I grew up on the movies (not films, movies). I believe in the collective dream world that is Hollywood. It is still an ideal for me.

Accommodation, or the portrait of the client and the place?

– Bob, there is a part of your work that is accommodating and

flattering to the tastes of the client. I would say the Bancho House is an example in which you try to camouflage your building so that it is perfectly acceptable within its context. What I would call, after David Riesman, a kind of 'other directed architecture'.

There are agendas that clients have, and agendas that architects have, and when these come together you can make something that is interesting, important even. Perhaps there is deeper meaning than you are willing to admit in my willingness to sympathetically interpret my client's wishes. I do not think a building should flaunt its ironies, and certainly the architect should not broadcast theory. They are for the public to discover. In any case, Bancho House is a first effort on my part to understand and express the very modern dilemma posed by the synthesis of two extremely different, yet increasingly intersecting cultures; those of Japan and the United States, or on a more fundamental level, of the Orient and the Occident. Can architecture help to build bridges across cultures that are seen in some ways to be unbridgeable? Can it illuminate ironies that make the attempt so difficult, so challenging and so worth the effort? There are many ironies in the design of Bancho House but they are deeper and more complicated than you propose.

– I haven't seen any ironies in the Bancho House.

You haven't met the client; you haven't seen the site; you haven't asked me to describe the process of our work; you've merely looked at a watercolour rendering.

– But you are designing a sort of Georgian, British residential architecture.

Let me try and describe the building and its circumstances: the owner is an internationally minded Japanese businessman who was educated in an American boarding school and at MIT before World War Two. He admires things Anglo-American, in particular the English-inspired vernacular of our 1930s Colonial-style work. Shortly after the cessation of hostilities in 1945, our client built a house on the site which, as the property values escalated and the neighbourhood became urbanised, he demolished to make way for Bancho House: a building containing five floors of offices and a two-storey penthouse apartment that he and his wife will live in.

The site is across the street from the British Embassy, a lushly landscaped compound of Soane-inspired villa-like buildings constructed between the two world wars.

– People see it as ersatz.

Ersatz what? I think what we have built is quite the opposite: it is an absolutely sincere effort to represent a complicated situation. There is a middle ground: one I believe to be more 'honest' to the situation. It can't be avoided in the commercial sector, not even by so puristic an architect as Tadao Ando. In two of Ando's buildings that I've visited – one in Tokyo, one in Kyoto – I was amazed to discover discos and neon, and all sorts of worldly things, transforming what were conceived as austere environments. What does it all mean? What is the function of degree-zero architecture in our hotted up, post-industrial world?

– That is a different kind of problem. I agree that Ando's work is out of phase with its content. But I would like to save the 'Bob the First, Second and Third' from 'Bob the Fourth'. 'Bob the Fourth', I would say, is a little too accommodating to the tastes of the client, from time to time.

I try not to confuse architecture with politics or social reform or theology . . . My purpose is not to sit in judgement – to comment yes, but not to judge.

– Architects should also raise consciousness.

They should bring quality! Architecture is not a form of applied ethics or politics – which is not to say that architects are not exempt from ethical and moral standards. But I object to the sermonising of the left and the sermonising of the right. I find the *zeitgeist*-driven pontification of the Modernists as tendentious as the God-given moralising of the Classicists. Architecture is neither the product of the class struggle nor the eleventh commandment; it is the art of

building well, and the art of building meaningfully. The older I get, the more I judge buildings from the past and from our own time, by considering how *well* they gave form to the building's literal and symbolic functions. Architecture is not an interior monologue shared with an audience; it is not a self-portrait; if anything, it is a portrait of a client (programme) and a place (site, cultural context).

– Quality also raises consciousness – that I wouldn't dispute. I hope we don't get into an either/or situation. But quality is not a substitute for the sublimation of political and social issues.

I don't sublimate them, I don't flaunt them; I think critics should read deeper than the surface.

– Well now that you have told me how the Bancho House is ironic I suppose I'll have to wait until its execution to judge for myself.

Bancho House, for all its investigation of traditional form, is a very modern building: not only in its programme as an office building, or in its earthquake resistant construction, but in its details – which are completely re-thought in relationship to a technology of glass and thin-sliced stone. Our building is to Soane as Soane was to the ancients – a creative interpretation made out of love for the past, and respect for the present. Modernism is one thing; modernity another. I am for modernity which is not judgemental or abstractly ideal, but existential and accommodating and real.

On Post-Modernism

– But Stirling and Botta generally make a juxtaposition between the Classical and Modern language. They make inversions, tensions and conflicts, and at Stuttgart Stirling doesn't even try to resolve them. He says there is no way these two cultures can be resolved, and so it is not up to him to do it. These cultures are in conflict and he is making a symbolic ornament out of that, a drama. Venturi, Norberg-Schultz, myself, and Lyotard, all agree that Post-Modernism is about the plurality of discontinuous languages. Stirling confronts them and makes a drama out of this, whereas I would say that in your accommodating phase, you sublimate this.

James Stirling has designed a wonderful building at Stuttgart, and I think he has addressed the related issues of Modernism and modernity brilliantly, but I think there are other ways to address the same issues. We must move on in life. I am as interested at this moment in continuities as discontinuities, perhaps even more in the continuities. But I recognise that seamless continuities between past and present are not now, nor never have been possible – at least not since the beginning of modern times in the Renaissance.

– One of the nicest things you have ever written is the essay The Doubles of Post-Modern. *I find it very creative and investigative scholarship of the highest level. You distinguish between the 'schismatic' and 'traditional' Post-Modernism – I think you only miss calling the 'schismatic' variety Late-Modernism – but those are my labels. The first question is; have you left Post-Modernism as you were defining it then; or do you see yourself carrying forward some kind of Post-Modern agenda?*

I think Post-Modernism makes its contribution as a critique of Modernism. Ideally, Post-Modernism describes an intellectual and cultural movement, like Romanticism, capable of sustaining many different modes of expression. But, regrettably, Post-Modernism has given rise to a substyle: a kind of cartoon Classicism, if you will. But once you get past this least significant level there is something far more profound to chew on. There is nothing being done in architecture today, that doesn't in some way operate on a level which could be called Post-Modernist. We are in a postmodernist era. Having transgressed the line from Modernism to Post-Modernism, we really don't need to talk about it anymore. Let's get on with it. I just say that we have architecture again, and enjoy the freedom to make buildings as we deem them appropriate, and not as representations of a supervening, *a priori* cultural-political critique.

The war against exclusive ideologies is over; let us enjoy the peace. We are now free to live with the past, to connect up with a continuing culture of architecture, and for me that includes the culture of Modernism as well. Perhaps it is for the critics to debate, but I feel I have made a contribution to understanding. Let's become scholar architects once again. Let us research the work of the past – even the work of the Modernists – and reassess it, use it in relationship to our own work. For me, that is the greatest liberation, the pleasure of architecture. I became an architect because I loved the buildings I knew first-hand and the ones I got to know in books; I did not become an architect because I was a failed political scientist, or economist or engineer. Post-Modernism, in my view, serves as a way to get beyond the false barriers raised by the Modernists, to a much broader view of history and of what we can do as architects.

– *For me, Post-Modernism is much larger than that. A lot of the young feel that there must be a 'critical' or a 'radical' Post-Modernism.*

I think it is very hard to be radical in that sense anymore, because the media swallows up new, even contrary ideas so quickly. The radical loses its edge. But to be critical – in the sense of evaluative – both of presentation and aesthetics, is essential. But the critical stance does not necessarily imply Establishment-bashing; though I recognise that as I get older and, I suppose, more successful, I become part of the Establishment, so this must sound self-serving. But then again – you're not getting any younger yourself! In any case, I welcome the younger generation's enthusiasm for the Modernist work of the past – so long as it is not at the expense of the wider, deeper traditions of architecture, and so long as it has a critical edge to it. I very much enjoy the reinterpretive, nostalgia-filled games of Morphosis or Holl or Tschumi, whose play with the Modernism of the 1920s helps us all towards a synthesis between the extremes of 20th-century architecture: anti-traditional Modernism and anti-Modernist traditionalism. I see Post-Modernism's programme as that of synthesis, rather than the programme of schism that was Modernism's. That's what I argued for in *The Doubles of Post-Modern.*

– *What Hal Foster and others are saying is that accommodating Post-Modernism has been absorbed by a consumer society. When you wished to be in the Deconstruction show, you showed the tensions in yourself.*

The juxtaposition of discontinuous forms is an artistic possibility which I have explored time and again in my work, from the Greenwich and Westchester houses of the 1970s, to the very recent Mexx Headquarters and the competition for the Science Academy in Berlin, where the discontinuities were spatial and tectonic and between modes of expression as well. Post-Modernism has *made* its point; it is now possible to reshuffle the historical deck – to construct and reconstruct the past. The reconsideration of the role of the architect *vis à vis* mass society, that the Modernists undertook in the 1920s was liberating, but no more a final solution than any other historical style.

Space, Light and Representation

– *What do you see as* your *most important contribution? Which do you think are your best buildings? Do you think about your past, like Peter Eisenman does?*

Well, I'm not as obsessive as Peter.

– *You don't have two psychoanalysts?*

I don't even have one – maybe I should! Of my earliest architecture, the Lang House is very important. It initiated a line of investigation that led me to the BEST Products facade and now to the Disney Casting Building. Then there are always the shingle houses, the simplicity and straightforwardness of which, I hope make clear that one can build with dignity even today.

– *Your Shingle Style houses are your most mature work.*

I have been able to build more of them than any other type,

therefore I have been able to dig more deeply into the form language, the issues of composition, detailing, character, what have you. Because they participate in a deep and widely respected cultural tradition, and are largely divorced from the public realm, they are able to be quite consistent.

– *But they can turn into the 'Edwardian Accommodating'.*

You are changing the ground under me. You are asking me a question, then answering it; a famous Charles Jencks trick.

– *I have always said your tower for the* Chicago Tribune *Competition, 1980, was the most radical skyscraper design of its time. I may be overrating this scheme, but it is more polychromatic than anything of Cesar Pelli's. Who helped you with it, was it Gavin McRae Gibson?*

Yes, Gavin worked on that. And, no, you are not overrating it. It is good, and provocative, and has been influential.

– *That is a very inventive design both formally and conceptually. It is a building that raised consciousness, a project one would put with the 20 canonic schemes that changed Post-Modern Architecture.*

The basic assumption of the *Tribune* scheme was to provoke. In a competition you can be very free, especially in one held for a building that was never to be built. I designed the tower in context: in the context of the iconic, tall buildings I love from the 1920s, and in the context of the 1922 *Tribune* Competition itself. I also designed it as a challenge to those who could not see the place of symbolism and scenography in tall commercial architecture, and those who said that 'new' materials – glass especially – negated the representational function of architectural form. What was done was to take on the scheme that almost everyone had made fun of since the 1920s – the entry of Adolf Loos. Whenever I had read about the competition, or heard a lecture, fun was made of Loos' entry, yet the more I thought about it, the more it seemed to me that Loos had the right idea all along.

– *Any other canonic buildings? You have mentioned the Disney Project?*

Disney is too new for me to know if it will be 'canonic' – such a term – but it carries forward the stream of thinking that up to now, I have mostly explored in unrealised projects. It comes out of my thinking about Frank Lloyd Wright, particularly the Marin County Center, with its split circulation and suggestive imagery.

– *But you know, funnily enough I like your work which is unresolved and is pushing ideas and not afraid to take chances.*

I am not searching for a universal theory. I am preoccupied with the here and now – especially with the situation of art and culture in America, a place with no real history except for what has been invented or imparted in just over 200 years.

– *One of the things which I find really interesting in your work is the handling of space and light; for instance the conversion of a dining hall in Virginia.*

It is not just a conversion. True the inside of two 10-year-old shed-roofed dining halls were gutted, but the entire building was extended on its two principal facades to accommodate an additional 200 hundred diners. What you see from the outside are the new ranges of the expanded building, consisting of four pavilions, and together forming a new perimeter. The glass walls, the pyramid roofs, and the arcades are all new constructions added to the building.

– *That has the best qualities of your handling of space and light. The light obviously related to the lanterns of Soane, and Louis Kahn.*

Jefferson, in some ways the American Soane, is the site-specific local reference; Kahn is the contemporary reference. His Trenton Bath Houses made an incredible impression on me when I first saw them around 1960, and much as I could never stand them as buildings – the quality of construction was so poor – I found them incomparable as compositions, as exemplars of the Classical ideal.

– I find your plans sometimes more interesting than your elevations.

I think that is probably the problem of the Modernist still in me.

– For instance, the residence at Hewlett Harbour has marvellous lighting elements – partly taken from Lutyens, and partly developing out of Shingle Style space. But its elevation – four engaged Ionic columns with plinths on top – is taken from the Ashmolean Museum in Oxford. And this isn't even a public building; it just flatters the tastes of the client. But in the plan, I have never seen such wonderful handlings of stairs. The stairs make me swoon. Indeed your stairways and entrances are the nicest of the 80s.

Oh so you *do* understand my work, you do understand its virtues and my interests. What you are talking about is not the plans but the space. I'm pleased. I'm not sure whether a critic flattering an architect is good or bad – I think it's probably good. But in any case, I just love the facades of Soane and Cockerell, and was happy for the opportunity to make them my own, as it were. I think there is a wonderful rhetorical dimension in architecture that is too little explored: it is a rhetoric of 'taste' and it needs to be vented from time to time. To me, the ultimate vulgarity in architecture is not the fulsome exploration of form, but the false pretensions of minimalism; of loft-like settings with affluent people sitting around on tortured metalwork, debating million-dollar paintings – the kind of Modernist pretensions Tom Wolfe has exposed. So vulgarity is in the mindset of the beholder: it is in no way an absolute.

– The residence at Marblehead is one of your great Edwardian Shingle Style solutions.

You shouldn't call it Edwardian, it just doesn't make much sense in the American context. Just call it a great Shingle Style house.

– It could be Newport 1890.

Or HH Richardson in the Boston suburbs, which was really the reference.

– The handling of the stairs creates a very convincing spatial sequence – including the inglenook to the left of the living room.

One of the reasons this house is successful, aside from what you have mentioned, is that it is the product of a series of excruciatingly tight pressures of sight, view and topography. When you have a flat piece of land you can be much looser: I think you and I both like this house because it has that tight-fit plan.

– And because it is solving a limited problem without too much money and too free a hand. It is like Borromini, who liked to design in tight corners. I also find that your smaller, tighter solutions are more interesting. I am again upset by your villa in New Jersey. It is much more interesting in plan than in elevation, and I cannot understand why you have the roof pushed down so close to the top

floor, squashing the top window that needed another two feet.

You have raised this point before.

– But you didn't answer me. Why is the roof squeezing the top window? Why are the proportions so constricted? Charles Platt would never have done that.

I was probably thinking as much about Frank Lloyd Wright as Charles Platt; more, even. Wright's Winslow House establishes conclusively that the Prairie Style did not grow out of a prairie vernacular but out of the tradition of the Tuscan villa. I suppose the roof is pushed down, as you would have it, and the details simplified to give the house a sleekness and compaction that still seems 'modern' to me.

– Going back to the roof; the functional answer is that it shades those top windows.

The compositional answer is that there is a great tension between the roof and the windows which I like.

– Conceptually it is a glazed layer.

The idea of the house perhaps came from a villa I once saw in a photo, where the loggia had been glazed to protect the frescoes. I don't remember which villa or where, but the glass was put in very sensitively, probably in the 19th century. It is much like the effect discussed endlessly in Modernism, of the wall being pulled free of the structure. Can we mix traditional vocabulary with the openness that comes from a Modernist view of the world? I love the tension of a wall that is completely glazed but also has a constructed aspect; a real sense of closure. It is not glass as a negative but glass as a positive. The other thing that is important about this house is the organising of the whole landscape: the lesson that comes from Lutyens, a large part of whose greatness lies in his ability to make the architecture of the land and the architecture of the house – one. Platt produced beautiful gardens, but he is nowhere near Lutyens in the geometrical discipline of his houses or his sites. You probably disagree, but history won't prove you correct.

– Lutyens was the greater architect, I would not begin to dispute that. One of the things about a cosmopolite architect in an era when Modernism is trying to be reborn is the question of authenticity and sincerity. When will the real Bob Stern stand up? When the real Bob Stern stands up, part of him will remain sitting because of his relationship with so many other periods and so many other authors. By definition you are ideologically committed to continuities, particularly the continuity of history. You bind the past, the present and the future together in a way which I try in my own writings. It's a position you are heading towards as are Charles Vandenhove and Kisho Kurokawa, who both bind time in a seamless web.

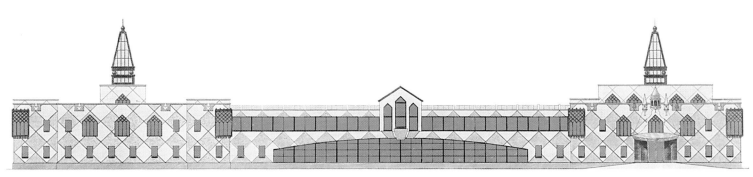

P 130: BANCHO HOUSE, TOKYO, JAPAN, 1988-89; *ABOVE*: CASTING CENTER, WALT DISNEY WORLD, 1987-89

PROJECT CREDITS

Lang Residence, 1973-74
Assistant-in-Charge: Jeremy P Lang. Assistant: Edmund H Stoecklein. Landscape Architect: Daniel Stewart.

Westchester County Residence, 1974-76
Assistants-in-Charge: Daniel L Colbert, Jeremy P Lang. Assistants: Robert Buford, Joan Chan, Ronne Fisher. Interior Design Associate: Ronne Fisher.

New York Townhouse, 1975
Assistant-in-Charge: Jeremy P Lang. Assistants: Wayne Berg, Ronne Fisher, Laurence Marner.

Roosevelt Island Housing, 1975
Assistant-in-Charge: Wayne Berg. Assistants: Robert Buford, Daniel L Colbert, Gregory Gall, Jeremy P Lang, Laurence Marner, Joan Oxenfelt, Edmund H Stoecklein, Clifford M Thacher-Renshaw.

Subway Suburb, 1976
Assistants: Mark Albert, Wayne Berg, Edmund H Stocklein, Charles D Warren.

Lawson Residence, 1979-81
Architect-in-Charge: John Averitt. Assistants: Terry Brown, John Krieble. Charles D Warren.

Residence in Llewellyn Park, 1979-81
Assistant-in-Charge: Anthony Cohn. Assistants: Ethelind Coblin, Alan J Gerber, Gavin Macrae-Gibson.

Residence in Chilmark, 1979-83
Architect-in-Charge: Roger H Seifter. Senior Assistant: John Krieble. Interior Design Associate: Alan J Gerber.

***Chicago Tribune* Tower, 1980**
Assistant-in-Charge: Gavin Macrae-Gibson. Assistants: Mark Albert, Charles D Warren.

Farm Neck Residence, 1980-83
Architect-in-Charge: Roger H Seifter. Assistant: John Krieble. Interior Design Associate: Ronne Fisher.

Residence in East Hampton, 1980-83
Assistant-in-Charge: Roger H Seifter Assistant: Terry Brown. Interior Design Associate: Ronne Fisher.

Observatory Hill Dining Hall, University of Virginia, 1982-84
Architect-in-Charge: Roger H Seifter. Senior Assistant: Thomas A Kligerman.

Brooklyn Residence, 1983
Architect-in-Charge: Alan J Gerber Assistants: Anthony Cohn, David Eastman, William T Georgis, Warren A James, Kristin McMahon. Interior Design Associate: Alan J Gerber. Landscape Associate: Robert Ermerins.

Kentucky Farmhouse, 1983
Assistant-in-Charge: Paul L Whalen. Assistants: Gregory Gilmartin, Oscar Shamamian, Mark Wade.

Point West Place, 1983-85
Architect-in-Charge: John Ike. Assistants: Stephen TB Falatko, Peter Merwin, Thai Nguyen, Luis Rueda, Mariko Takahashi, Graham S Wyatt.

Villa in New Jersey, 1983-89
Assistant-in-Charge: Thomas A Kligerman. Assistants: Augusta Barone, Victoria Gasasco, Arthur Chabon, Berndt Dams, William T Georgis, Natalie Jacobs, Laurie Kerr, Francoise Sogno. Landscape Associate: Robert Ermerins. Interior Design Assistants: Ingrid Armstrong, Stephan Johnson, Tanya Kelly, Lisa Maurer.

Residence at Calf Creek, 1984-87
Architect-in-Charge: Amanda Le Gardeur. Assistant: Luis Rueda-Salazar. Landscape Associate: Robert Ermerins. Interior Design Associate: Lisa Maurer.

Sunstone, Quogue, 1984-87
Assistant-in-Charge: Randy M Correll. Assistants: Thomas Nohr, Constance Treadwell.

Marblehead Residence, 1984-87
Architect-in-Charge: Roger H Seifter. Senior Assistant: Caroline Hancock. Assistants: Kaarin Taipale.

Hewlett Harbour, 1984-88
Architect-in-Charge: Charles Warren. Assistants: Re Hagele, Grant Marani, Jenny Peng, Elizabeth Thompson. Landscape Associate: Robert Ermerins. Interior Design Associate: Lisa Maurer.

Architect's Offices, New York, 1985
Assistants-in-Charge: Anthony Cohn, Thomas Nohr. Assistant: Caryl Kinsey.

Mexx International Headquarters, The Netherlands, 1985-87
Assistant-in-Charge: Graham S Wyatt. Assistants: Preston J Gumberich, William C Nolan, Jenny Peng, Jeff Schofield, Pat Tiné. Landscape Associate: Robert Ermerins.

Kol Israel Synagogue, 1985-89
Architect-in-Charge: Thomas A Kligerman. Project Associate: Caryl Kinsey. Assistants: Augusta Barone, Victoria Casasco, Peter Dick, Michelle Huot, Laurie Kerr, Timothy E Lenahan, Jeff Wilkinson.

Russian Hill Residence, 1985-89
Associate-in-Charge: Alan J Gerber. Project Associates: Kristin McMahon, Elizabeth Thompson. Assistant: Ken McIntyre-Horito.

Tegeler Hafen, Berlin, 1985-89
Architect-in-Charge: Graham S Wyatt. Assistants: Ellen Kenyon Coxe, Paul B Williger.

Master Plan and Studio IV, University of California, 1986-89
Architect-in-Charge: Graham S Wyatt. Assistants: Preston J Gumberich, Alexander P Lamis, Jeff Schofield.

Grand Harbour, 1986-89
Architect-in-Charge: Paul L Whalen. Assistants: John Berson, Chris Blake, Sonia Chao, Alexis O Fernandez, Michelle Huot, Warren A James, Laurie Kerr, Dan Lobitz, William Nolan, Karen Okazaki, Anthony Poon.

222 Berkeley Street, 1986-91
Associate-in-Charge: Ellen K Cox, Barry Rice. Project Associate: Thomas M Eisele. Design Phase Associates: Anthony Cohn, Timothy E Lenahan. Assistants: Keller A Easterling, Sandra L Parsons, Elizabeth A Valella.

Disney Casting Center, 1987-89
Architect-in-Charge: John Ike. Project Associate: Barry Rice. Assistants: Augusta Barone, Austin Brown, Luis Fontcuberta, Michael Jones, Scott Shin.

Pasadena Police Building, 1987-90
Principals-in-Charge: Robert AM Stern, Christ J Kamages. Project Manager: Timothy L Craig. Project Architects: Karen Gibb, John Ike, Barry Rice. Project Team: Carlos Abruzzese, Augusta Barone, Austin Brown, Robin Burr, Timothy E Lenahan, Jane Marshall, Fakoor Popal, Michael Radcliffe, Jeff Schofield, Scott Shin.

Ohstrom Library, 1987-91
Architect-in-Charge: Graham S Wyatt. Project Managers: Preston J Gumberich, Caryl Kinsey. Design Phase Associate: Charles D Warren. Assistants: Abigail M Huffman, Timothy E Lenahan, Sandra L Parsons, Sharon Pett, Eva Pohlen, Mary Ellen Stenger. Interior Design Associate: Lisa Maurer. Assistant: Alice Yiu. Landscape Associate: Robert Ermerins. Assistant: William C Skelsey.

Bancho House, Tokyo, 1988-89
Architect-in-Charge: Grant Marani. Assistants: W David Henderson, Mabel O Wilson. Interior Design Associate: Raul Morillas. Assistants: Deborah Emery, Sharon Pett.

Two Venture Plaza, 1988-90
Architects-in-Charge: John Ike, Thomas A Kligerman. Senior Assistant: Michael Jones.

'PSFS: Beaux Arts Theory and Rational Expressionism', *Journal of the Society of Architectural Historians*, May 1962, pp 84-102.
'Relevance of the Decade 1929-1939', *Journal of the Society of Architectural Historians*, March 1965.
Perspecta, the Yale Architectural Journal 9/10, Guest Editor, 1965.
'Constitution Plaza One Year After', *Progressive Architecture*, December 1965, pp 166-71.
40 Under 40: Young Talent in Architecture, Exhibition Catalolgue, American Federation of Arts, New York, 1966.
New Directions in American Architecture, Brinziller, New York, 1969; expanded 2nd edition 1977.
'Yale 1950-65', *Oppositions 4*, October 1974, pp 35-62.
George Howe: Towards a Modern American Architecture, Yale University Press, New Haven, 1975.
'Toward an Architecture of Symbolic Assemblage', *Progressive Architecture*, April 1975, pp 72-77.
Architecture and Urbanism, Guest Editor, (Special Feature, 'White and Gray), Tokyo, April 1975, pp 25-180.
'A Serious Discussion of an Almost Whimsical House', *Architectural Record*, July 1975, pp 99-104.
'Gray Architecture: Quelques Variations Post-Modernistes Autour de l'Orthodoxie', *l'Architecture d'Aujourd'hui*, Paris, August/September 1976, p 83.
Foreword, with Wilder Green, David Gebhard and Deborah Nevins, *200 Years of American Architectural Drawing*, New York, Whitney Library of Design, 1977.
A+U, Guest Editor, (Special Feature '40 Under 40+10'), Tokyo, January 1977.
'At the Edges of Modernism', *Architectural Design*, vol 47, no 4, April 1977, pp 274-286.
'Further Thoughts on Millbank', *Architectural Design*, with George Baird and Charles Jencks, no 47, July/August 1977, pp 543-544.
'Venturi and Rauch: Learning to Love Them', *Architectural Monographs*, vol 1 (1978), pp 93-94.

'New Directions in Modern American Architecture, Postscript', *Architectural Association Quarterly*, vol 9, nos 2 & 3, 1978, pp 93-94.
'The Suburban Alternative: Coping with the Middle City', *Architectural Record*, August 1978, pp 93-100.
'How to Redesign New York', *Art News*, vol 78, No 9, November 1978, pp 81-82.
'Drawings from Models', with Frances Halsband, RM Kliment and Richard B Oliver, *Journal of Architectural Education*, vol XXXII No 1, September 1978, p 7.
Commentary, *Philip Johnson: Collected Writings*, Oxford University Press, New York, 1979.
The Architect's Eye: American Architectural Drawings from 1799-1979, co-authored with Deborah Nevins, Pantheon, New York, 1979.
'Doubles of Post-Modern', *Harvard Architectural Review*, vol 1, Spring 1980, pp 74-87.
'After the Modern Movement', *Parametro*, No 72, pp 36-40.
'With Rhetoric: The New York Apartment House' *VIA*, vol IV, 1980, pp 78-111.
'Post Profligate Architecture – Some Observations in the Waning of the Petroleum Era', *American Architecture After Modernism A+U* Special Issue, March 1981, pp 8-15.
The Anglo-American Suburb, with John M Massengale, Academy Editions, London, 1981.
'American Architecture After Modernism', *A+U*, Guest Editor of Special Issue, March 1981.
'Architecture, History, and Historiography at the End of the Modernist Era', *History in, of, and for Archticture*, in John E Hancock, ed, Rizzoli International Publications Inc, New York, 1981, pp 34-43.
'Modernismus und Postmodernismus', *Design 1st Unsichtbar*, Locker Verlag, Vienna, 1981, pp 259-271.
'Notes on Post-Modernism', *Yale Seminars in Architecture*, Yale University Press, New Haven, Connecticut, 1981, pp 1-35.
'Human Scale at the End of the age of Modernism', *Collaboration:*

Artists and Architects, Whiney Library of Design, New York, 1981, pp 114-115.
'Setting the Stage: Herts and Tallant', with John M Massengale and Gregory Gilmartin, *Skyline*, December 1981, pp 32-33.
'Toward an Urban Suburbia, Once Again Suburban Enclaves' *Cities*, 1982, pp 32-33, 79.
'International Style: Immediate Effects', *Progressive Architecture*, Febuary 1982, pp 106-109.
Raymond Hood, with Thomas P Catalano, Institute of Architecture and Urban Studies and Rizzoli International Publications Inc, New York, 1982.
East Hampton's Heritage: An Illustrated Architectural Record, with Clay Lancaster and Robert Hefner, WW Norton & Company, Inc, 1982.
'Beginnings', *A+U*, July 1982 Extra Edition, pp 13-16.
New York 1900, with John M Massengale and Gregory Gilmartin, Rizzoli International Publications Inc, New York, 1983.
'After the Modern Period', *Forum 29*, No 2, Amsterdam, 1984-85, pp 54-55.
'Four Towers', *A+U*, January 1985, 'On Style, Classicism and Pedagogy', *Precis 5*, Fall 1984, pp 16-23.
Editor, *International Design Yearbook 1985/86*, BV Uitgevermaatschappij Elsevier, Amsterdam/Brussels and Abbeyville Press, New York, 1985.
'Modern Traditionalism' in Luis F Rueda, ed, *Robert AM Stern: Buildings and Projects 1981-1985*, Rizzoli International Publications, New York, 1986, pp 6-7.
'The American Street', in *Stirrings of Culture: Essays from the Dallas Institute*, eds Robert J Sardello and Gail Thomas, Dallas Institute Publications, 1986, pp 189-90.
'Designing the American Dream', *Architectural Digest 43*, April 1986, pp 30, 33, 35, 38.
'Images of an Ideal House', *House Beautiful 128*, June 1986, pp 111.
'Urbanismo Classico', *On: Diseno*, Barcelona, December 1986, pp 114-17.
American Architecture: Innovation and Tradition, Edited with David

G De Long and Helen Searing, Rizzoli International Publications, New York, 1986.
New York 1930, with Gregory Gilmartin and Thomas Mellins, assisted by David Fishman and Raymond W Gastil, Rizzoli International Publications, New York, 1987.
'Regionalism and the Continuity of Tradition' *CENTER: A Journal for Architecture in America 3*, 1987, pp 58-63.
'Travel Notes: Robert AM Stern', *Architectural Digest*, June 1987, pp 234, 238, 240, 243, 245, 247.
Modern Classicism, with Raymond Gastil, Rizzoli Internation Publication, New York, 1988.
Images of Fin-de-Siècle Architecture and Interior Decoration, Riiichi Miyake, forewood by Robert AM Stern, Kodansha International, Tokyo, Harper and Row, New York, 1988.
'Design as Emulation', *Architectural Design*, vol 58, no 9/10, 1988, pp 9-10, 20-23.
'New Yorkers . . . What about the City do you Cherish, What do you Hate, and what do you Miss?', respondents include Robert AM Stern, *Architecture: The AIA Journal*, vol 77 no 4, April 1988, pp 57-97.
'An Architect's Impressions of Spain', *Architectural Digest*, vol 46, no 3, March 1989, p 128.
Perspecta: the First Twenty Five: a celebration of twenty five issues of Perspecta: the Yale Architectural Journal, Yale University, 1989.
'Housing America', with Tom Mellins, *Architectural Record*, vol 179, no 7, July 1991, pp 158-61.

Monographs
David Dunster, ed, *Robert Stern*, Academy Editions, London, 1981.
Peter Arnell and Ted Bickford, eds, *Robert AM Stern, Buildings and Projects 1965-1980*, Rizzoli International Publications, Inc, New York, 1981.
Toshio Nakamura, ed, 'The Residential Works of Robert AM Stern', *A+U*, July 1982, Extra Edition.
Luis F Rueda, ed, *Robert AM Stern: Buildings and Projects 1981-1985*, Rizzoli International, 1986.

ROBERT AM STERN; BUILDINGS AND PROJECTS

Wiseman House
Montauk, New York
1965-67

Tower Apartment
New York, New York
1966

Apartment for Mr and Mrs Robert
AM Stern
New York, New York
1967-68

Apartment for Mr. and Mrs. Robert
B Gimbe
New York, New York
1968

Stern Residence
East Hampton, New York
1968-69

Seiniger House
1969 (Project)

Showroom for Tiffeau-Busch, Ltd
New York, New York
1969

Showrooms for Charlie's Girls and
Hang Ten
New York, New York
1969

Jenkins Residence
East Hampton, New York
1969-70 (Project)

Sommerfield Apartment
New York, New York
1969-70

Two Projects for an Office Addition
Long Island, New York
1969-70

Kozmopolitan Gallery
New York, New York
1970 (Project)

Another Chance for Cities
Travelling Exhibition
1970

Danziger Poolhouse
Purchase, New York
1970-71

Geary Brownstone
New York, New York
1971 (Project)

Kardon Residence
Gladwynne, Pennsylvania
1971

Roberts Apartment
New York, New York
1971

White/Hoffman Duplex Apartment
Central Park West, New York
1971

Beebe Residence and Outbuildings
Montauk, New York
1971-72

Kretchmer Apartment
New York, New York
1972

Millstein Brownstone
New York, New York
1972-79

Architect's Office
New York
1973

Duplex Apartment
950 Fifth Avenue
New York City
1973

House Beautiful Living Center
1973

Howard Apartment
New York, New York
1973

Remodelled Farmhouse
Greenwich, Connecticut
1973

Rooftop Apartment
New York, New York
1973

Lang Residence
Washington, Connecticut
1973-74

Poolhouse
Greenwich, Connecticut
1973-74

Offices for Source Securities, Inc
New York, New York
1973-75

Café and Lounge
Ferris Booth Hall
Columbia University
New York, New York
1974 (Project)

Ferris Booth Hall Renovation
Columbia University
New York, New York
1980

Library, Community Museum and
Civic Square
Biloxi, Mississippi
1974 (Competition)

Middleton Apartment
New York, New York
1974

Model Apartment, Olympic Tower
New York, New York
1974

Residence and Outbuildings
Westchester County, New York
1974-76

Downtown Urban Development
Regina, Saskatchewan, Canada
1975 (Competition)

Hope Solinger Apartment
New York, New York
1975

Jerome Greene Hall
Columbia University
New York, New York
1975

Kastner Apartment
Elkins Park, Pennsylvania
1975

New York Townhouse
New York, New York
1975

Residence
East Hampton, New York
1975

Residence
North Stamford, Connecticut
1975

Roosevelt Island Competition
New York, New York
1975

Points of View
Mount Desert Island, Maine
1975-76

Carriage House
East Hampton, New York
1975-77

Association House Apartments
New York, New York
1976 (Project)

Peaceable Kingdom Barn
Texas
1976 (Project)

Subway Suburb
1976 (Project)

Killington Ski Lodge
Killington, Vermont
1976 (Competition)

State Capitol Annex Building
St Paul, Minnesota
1976 (Competition)

Riviera Beach
Singer Island, Florida
1976 (Competition)

Housing for the Elderly
Long Island, New York
1976 (Competition)

Rodman Rockefeller Apartment
New York, New York
1976

Anniversary Poster, IAUS
1977

Park Avenue Apartment
New York, New York
1977

Residence
Fairfield County
1977-78 (Project)

Silvera Residence
Deal, New Jersey
1977-78

Fresh Café
New York, New York
1978 (Project)

Redtop Additions and Renovation
Dublin, New Hampshire
1978

Furniture Design
Griffin Table
1978-80

Brooks Residence
East Hampton, New York
1979 (Project)

Catalog Showroom
Best Products
1979 (Project)

Super Spa
Bathing Pavilion
1979 (Project)

Visitor's Center
Shaker Village, Kentucky
1979 (Project)

Cohen Apartment
New York, New York
1979 (Project)

Erbun Fabrics Showroom
New York, New York
1979

First Avenue Squash Club
New York, New York
1979

Hitzig Apartment
New York, New York
1979

Smetana Medical Suite
New York, New York
1979

Temple of Love
East Hampton, New York
1979

Cottage Renovation
East Hampton, New York
1979-

Meltzer Residence
King's Point, New York
1979-80 (Project)

Contractor's Offices
Long Island City, New York
1979-80

Inner Dune Residence
East Hampton, New York
1979-80

Lawson Residence
East Quogue, New York
1979-81

Residence
Llewellyn Park, New Jersey
1979-81

Residence at Chilmark
Martha's Vineyard, Massachusetts
1979-83

Catlin Residence
Greenwich, Connecticut
1980 (Project)

City Hall Annex
Cincinnati, Ohio
1980 (Project)

Late Entry, *Chicago Tribune*
Tower Competition
Chicago, Illinois
1980 (Project)

Library
San Juan Capistrano, California
1980 (Project)

Prototype Housing
1980 (Project)

Roizen House at Ram Island
Shelter Island, New York
1980 (Project)

Saper House Addition
Woodstock, New York
1980 (Project)

DOM Headquarters
Bruhl, Germany
1980 (Competition)

Garibaldi Meucci Museum
1980 (Competition)

Schmertz Residence Alterations
East Hampton, New York
1980

Modern Architecture
After Modernism
Pavilion, Forum Design
Linz, Austria
1980

Facade
La Strada Novissima
Biennale Facade
Venice, Italy
1980

Tuscan Table
1980

Scaling Modernism
with Robert Graham, 1980

Keith Residence
Locust Valley, New York
1980-81 (Project)

Three Houses for Corbel Properties
Cove Hollow Farm
East Hampton, New York
1980-83

Classical Duplex Apartment
New York, New York
1980-82

Bozzi Residence
East Hampton, New York
1980-83

Residence at Farm Neck
Martha's Vineyard, Massachusetts
1980-1983

Kalamazoo Center
Kalamazoo, Michigan
1981 (Project)

Millstein Residence
Napeague, New York
1981 (Project)

Park Avenue Duplex Apartment
New York, New York
1981 (Project)

Raymond Hood Exhibit
The Institute for Architecture and
Urban Studies
New York, New York
1981 (Project)

Richmond Center
Richmond, Virginia
1981 (Project)

Rothschild Apartment
New York, New York
1981 (Project)

Stone Douglass Residence
East Hampton, New York
1981 (Project)

Lincoln Squash Club
New York, New York
1981

Offices for Obstetrics and
Gynecologic Associates
New York, New York
1981

Patricof House
East Hampton, New York
1981

Young-Hoffman Exhibition
Chicago, Illinois
1981

Keith Residence
Mill Neck, New York
1981-82

Two Houses for Archdeacon
Developers
Aspen, Colorado
1981-82

Stuart House
Purchase, New York
1981-83

Showroom for Shaw-Walker, Inc
Merchandise Mart
Chicago, Illinois
1981-82

Showroom for Shaw-Walker, Inc
Pacific Design Center
Los Angeles, California
1982

Showroom for Shaw-Walker, Inc
Washington, DC
1982-83

Showroom for Shaw-Walker, Inc
New York, New York
1983

Six Houses at Mecox Fields
Bridgehampton, New York
1981-88

Anthony Fisher Residence
Napeague, New York
1982 (Project)

House at Seaview
Amagansett, New York
1982 (Project)

'Classical Corner'
for *House & Garden Magazine*
1982

Silvera Apartment
New York, New York
1982

Interiors for the Yacht Ondine VI
Ondine Yacht Charters
1982-83

Faulkner House Apartments
University of Virginia
Charlottesville, Virginia
1982 (Competition)

Sprigg Lane Dormitories
University of Virginia
Charlottesville, Virginia
1982-84

Observatory Hill Dining Hall
University of Virginia
Charlottesville, Virginia
1982-84

Residence in New Jersey
1982-84

Tableware for Swid-Powell
1982-85

Swid Powell Series II
1986-

St Andrews
A Jack Nicklaus Golf Community
Hastings-on-Hudson, New York
1982-86

Farmhouse
Oldham County, Kentucky
1983 (Project)

Fox Hollow Run
Chappaqua, New York
1983 (Project)

Greenhouse Apartments
Cherry Creek
Denver, Colorado
1983 (Project)

Meltzer House Renovation
Pound Ridge, New York
1983 (Project)

Performing Arts Center
Anchorage, Alaska
1983 (Project)

Residence
Pound Ridge, New York
1983 (Project)

Residence on Lake Agawam
Southampton, New York
1983 (Project)

Residence at West Tisbury
Martha's Vineyard, Massachusetts
1983 (Project)

Schweber Apartment
The Dakota
New York, New York
1983 (Project)

Additions to The New Orleans
Museum of Art
New Orleans, Louisiana
1983 (Competition)

Borden Carriage House Renovation
Rumson, New Jersey
1983

Dinner at Eight Carpet
for Furniture of the 20th Century
1983

Reading Room
International House
New York, New York
1983

Student Pub
International House
New York, New York
1984

San Remo Carpet
1983

Point West Place
Framingham, Massachusetts
1983-85

Prospect Point
La Jolla, California
1983-85

Residence at Hardscrabble
East Hampton, New York
1983-85

Treadway House
Southampton, New York
1983-85

Houses, Colfax at Beden's Brook
Skillman, New Jersey
1983-87

Residence
Brooklyn, New York
1983-86

Copperflagg Corporation
Residential Development
Staten Island, New York
1983-88

Villa in New Jersey
1983-89

Residence in Massachusetts
1983-90

Congregation Shaare Zion Addition
Brooklyn, New York
1984 (Project)

City Place
Providence, Rhode Island
1984 (Project)

Greenwood Village
Bakersfield, California
1984 (Project)

Hillcrest Square
San Diego, California
1984 (Project)

1992 Chicago World's Fair
with a National Design Team
Organised by SOM, Chicago/
William E Brazley & Associates
1984 (Project)

Preakness Hills Country Club
Wayne, New Jersey
1984 (Project)

Private High School
Brooklyn, New York
1984 (Project)

Residence at Cow Bay
Martha's Vineyard, Massachusetts
1984 (Project)

Residence at the Shores
Vero Beach, Florida
1984 (Project)

St Andrews Clubhouse
Hastings-on-Hudson, New York
1984 (Project)

Seaside Hotel
Seaside, Florida
1984 (Project)

Sephardic Study Center
Brooklyn, New York
1984 (Project)

Urban Villa
Brooklyn, New York
1984 (Project)

Architecture Building
Roger Williams College
Bristol, Rhode Island
1984 (Competition)

Civic Center
Escondido, California
1984 (Competition)

Cultural Arts Pavilion
Newport News, Virginia
1984 (Competition)

Classical Pool Pavilion
Deal, New Jersey
1984-85

Ekstract Residence
East Hampton, New York
1984-85

Penthouse Apartment
New York, New York
1984-85

Pool Atrium
Deal, New Jersey
1984-85

Residence at Scarsdale Heights
New York, New York
1984-86

Whitman Residence
Marblehead, Massachusetts
1984-87

Residence at Calf Creek
Watermill, New York
1984-87

Sunstone
Quogue, New York
1984-87

Two Newton Place
Newton, Massachusetts
1984-87

Residence
Hewlett Harbor, New York
1984-88

House in Cold Spring Harbor
Lloyd's Neck, New York
1985 (Project)

McGee Farm
Holmdel, New Jersey
1985 (Project)

Residence at Cove Beach
East Marion, New York
1985 (Project)

Residence Renovation
Green's Farm, Connecticut
1985 (Project)

Ronald McDonald House
New York, New York
1985 (Project)

Rye Brook Park
Westchester County, New York
1985 (Project)

Metairie Park Country Day School
New Orleans, Louisiana
1985 (Competition)

Municipal Center
Phoenix, Arizona
1985 (Competition)

Architect's Office
New York, New York
1985

The New American Home
Dallas, Texas
1985

Temporary Clubhouse
Swan Valley
Breckenridge, Colorado
1985

Russian Hill Townhouses
San Francisco, California
1985-

The Shops at Primrose Brook
Bernardsville, New Jersey
1985-

House in the Highlands
Seattle, Washington
1985-86 (Project)

Druker Company Executive Suite
Boston, Massachusetts
1985-86

Milwin Farm
Ocean Township, New Jersey
1985-86

Houses at the Hamptons
Lexington, Massachusetts
1985-87

Abbott Residence, Taylors Creek
Southampton, New York
1985-87 (Project)

International Headquarters
Mexx International, BV
Voorschoten, The Netherlands
1985-87

Mexx, USA, Inc
New York Fashion Showroom
New York, New York
1986-87

Mexx Retail Shop
150 Peter Cornelius Hoofstraat
Amsterdam, The Netherlands
1986-87

Alterations and Additions to the
Sunningdale Country Club
Scarsdale, New York
1985-88

Middlesea
East Hampton, New York
1985-88

Berggruen Residence, Russian Hill
San Francisco, California
1985-89

Kol Israel Synagogue
Brooklyn, New York
1985-89

Residence
Pottersville, New Jersey
1985-89

Residence
Elberon, New Jersey
1985-89

Urban Villa
Tegeler Hafen
Berlin, Germany
1985-89

Addition to the Colonnade Hotel
Boston, Massachusetts
1986 (Project)

Sheldon Memorial Library Addition
St. Paul's School
Concord, New Hampshire
1986 (Project)

Apartment House
Fan Pier Development
Boston, Massachusetts
1986 (Project)

Apartment Tower
Union Theological Seminary
120th Street and Broadway
New York, New York
1986 (Project)

Chadha Residence
Wassenaar, The Netherlands
1986 (Project)

Craftsman Farms
Parsippany, New Jersey
1986 (Project)

Essex Bay Estates
West Gloucester, Massachusetts
1986 (Project)

Ettl Farm Development
Princeton, New Jersey
1986 (Project)

Glastonbury Rental Housing
Glastonbury, Connecticut
1986 (Project)

Kiluna Farm Houses
North Hills, New York
1986 (Project)

Desert House
Phoenix, Arizona
1986 (Project)

Pershing Square, Los Angeles
Competition with the SWA Group
California
1986

Jewelry for Acme
1986

MacDougal Gardens
New York, New York
1986

Shapiro House
Cove Hollow Farm
East Hampton, New York
1986

Brooklyn Law School
250 Joralemon Street
Brooklyn, New York
1986-

The Center for Jewish Life
Princeton University
1986-

Residence at Edgarton
Martha's Vineyard, Massachusetts
1986-87

Residence on Prospect Avenue
Hartford, Connecticut
1986-87

Hubbard Apartment
New York, New York
1986-87

Residence in River Oaks I
Houston, Texas
1986-88 (Project)

Patricof Apartment
New York, New York
1986-88

The Shops at Somerset Square
140 Glastonbury Boulevard
Glastonbury, Connecticut
1986-88

Two Houses
Stamford, Connecticut
1986-88

Meadowbrook Forum II
Glen Curtis Blvd and Merrick Ave
Mitchel Field
Hempstead, New York
1986-89 (Project)

Fine Arts Village Master Plan and
Fine Arts Studio IV
University of California, Irvine
1986-89

Grand Harbor
Vero Beach, Florida
1986-89

House at Wilderness Point
Fishers Island, New York
1986-89

Residence at Conyers Farm
Greenwich, Connecticut
1986-89

Residence in Chestnut Hill
Massachusetts
1986-91

Two Twenty Two Berkeley Street
Boston, Massachusetts
1986-91

Townhouse Apartment
New York, New York
1987 (Project)

New Town
Orlando, Florida
1987 (Project)

Pigeon Cove
Rockport, Massachusetts
1987 (Project)

Ryan Residence
Winnetka, Illinois
1987 (Project)

Santa Agueda Resort
Gran Canaria
Canary Islands, Spain
1987 (Project)

Winchester Country Club
Winchester, Virginia
1987 (Project)

Akademie der Wissenschaften
Berlin
1987 (Competition)

Richmond Visitors' Center
Richmond, Virginia
Competition (First Prize)
1987

Sailors' Snug Harbor Music Halls
Competition Entry
1987

An Owligorical House
1987

Cap d'Akiya
Hayama, Japan
1987-

Decorative Arts for Munari Design
Associati
1987-

The Grace Estate
East Hampton, New York
1987-

The Norman Rockwell Museum
Stockbridge, Massachusetts
1987-

Woodlynne
Birmingham, Michigan
1987-

Claremont Tower
120 Claremont Avenue
New York, New York
1987-88 (Project)

42nd Street Development Project
New York, New York
1987-88 (Project)

Casting Center
Walt Disney World
Lake Buena Vista, Florida
1987-89

Kathryn & Shelby Cullom
Davis Hall
International House
New York, New York
1987-89

Offices for Capital Research Co
New York, New York
1987-89

Residence at Brainard Woods
West Hartford, Connecticut
1987-89

Police Headquarters Building
Pasadena, California
1987-90

Sky View
Aspen, Colorado
1987-90

Carnegie Hill Townhouse
New York, New York
1987-90

Yacht and Beach Club Resorts
Walt Disney World
Lake Buena Vista, Florida
1987-91

Ohrstrom Library
St Paul's School
Concord, New Hampshire
1987-91

Spruce Lodge
Old Snowmass, Colorado
1987-91

Arrowwood
Ryebrook, New York
1988 (Project)

Harborview
Baltimore, Maryland
1988 (Project)

University of California, Santa Cruz
Cottages 9 & 10
Masterplan and Design
1988 (Project)

Centro Cultural de Belem
Lisbon, Portugal
1988 (Competition)

First Government House
Sydney, Australia
1988 (Competition)

South Pointe Court
Miami Beach, Florida
1988 (Competition)

ARC Exhibition,
Tokyo, Japan
1988

Bergdorf Goodman Window
1988

California Lifeguard Tower
1988 (Project)

Table Lamp for The Lighthouse
Child Development Center
1988

Rizzoli Christmas Tree
1988

Bartholomew County Hospital
Columbus, Indiana
1988-

House at North York
Ontario, Canada
1988-

Ninety Tremont Street
St James Properties
Boston, Massachusetts
1988-

Nittsu Fujimi Land Golf Club
Izu Peninsula, Japan
1988-

High Camp Ski Lodge
Squaw Valley, USA
1988-

Bancho House
Tokyo, Japan
1988-89

Herrmann Apartment
New York, New York
1988-90

Two Venture Plaza
Irvine Center
Irvine, California
1988-90

Residence in River Oaks II
Houston, Texas
1988-91

Town Square – Wheaton
Wheaton, Illinois
1988-91

Hotel Cheyenne
Euro Disneyland
Marne La Vallée
France
1988 - 92

Newport Bay Club Hotel
Euro Disneyland
Marne La Vallée
France
1988-92

The Country Club
Villages at Rocky Fork
New Albany, Ohio
1989 (Project)

Gilliam Residence
Kiawah Island, South Carolina
1989 (Project)

Houses for Villages at Rocky Fork
New Albany, Ohio
1989 (Project)

Mar-a-Lago Apartment Building
Surfers Paradise
1989 (Project)

City Hall Complex
Orlando, Florida
1989 (Competition)

Morton Street Ventilation Building
Port Authority of NY and NJ
New York, New York
1989 (Competition)

United States Embassy
Cultural and Consular Building
Bajcsy Zsilinsky Ut
Budapest, Hungary
1989-

Apartment House, Chicago, Illinois
1989-

Bed and Bath Furnishings for
Altelier Martex
1989-

Concord Walk Hotel
Charleston, South Carolina
1989-

Furniture and Fabric Design
Hickory Business Furniture
1989-

Golf Club House at Somers
Westchester, New York
1989-

House on Georgica Cove
East Hampton, New York
1989-

Residence
Bel Air, California
1989-

Roger Tory Peterson Institute
Jamestown, New York
1989-

San Diego Riverwalk
San Diego, California
1989-

Kiawah Beach Club
Kiawah Island, South Carolina
1989-90 (Project)

Rowe Residence
Bloomfield Hills, Michigan
1989-90

Residence at Woodlynne
Bloomfield Hills, Michigan
1989-91

Washington State Labor and
Industries Building (Competition)
Olympia, Washington
1990

Espace Euro Disney
Villiers-sur-Marne,
France,
1990

Chiburi Lake Golf Resort
Chiburi, Japan
1990

Del Mar Civic Center
Del Mar, California
1990

Izumidai Resort
Izu Peninsula, Japan
1990

Kitsuregawa Golf Club House/Inn
Tochigi Prefecture, Japan
1990

Na Pali Haweo
Kamehame Ridge
Oahu, Hawaii,
1990-

Residence in Hunting Valley
Geauga County, Ohio
1990-

St Barnabas Memorial Garden
Irvington, New York
1990-

Shinshirakawa Resort
Shirakawa, Japan
1990-

The Turning Point
Rijksweg A-9 and Keerpuntweg
Amstelveen, The Netherlands
1990-

Denver Public Library
Denver, Colorado
1990-91 (Competition)

Banana Republic
744 N Michigan Avenue
Chicago, Illinois
1990-91

Parlor, DIFFA Showhouse
115 East 79th Street
New York, New York
1990-91

Mountain Residence
Yamanashi, Japan
1991-

Tivoli Apartments
Tokyo, Japan
1991